S0-BYA-181

Making the Church Work

Converting the Church for the 21st Century

My Book

Patricia Wilson-Kastner

Making the Church Work
Converting the Church for the 21st Century

Edward H. Hammett

SMYTH & HELWYS
PUBLISHING, INC.
Macon, Georgia

ISBN 1-57312-157-6

Making the Church Work
Converting the Church for the 21st Century

Edward H. Hammett

Copyright © 1997
Smyth & Helwys Publishing, Inc.
6316 Peake Road
Macon, Georgia 31210-3960
1-800-747-3016

All rights reserved.
Printed in the United States of America.

The paper used in this publication meets the minimum
requirements of American Standard for Information
Sciences—Permanence of Paper for
Printed Library Materials,
ANSI Z39.48-1984.

Library of Congress Cataloging-in-Publication

Hammett, Edward H.
    Making the church work:
    converting the church for the 21st century/
    Edward H. Hammett.
    xii + 116 pp.   6" x 9" (15 x 23 cm.)
    Includes bibliographical references.
    ISBN 1-57312-157-6   (alk. paper)
    1. Church renewal.
    2. Christianity—20th century.
    3. Christianity—Forecasting.
    I. Title.
    BV600.2.H275   1997
    262'001'7—dc21

                                        97-11345
                                        CIP

BV
600.2
.H275
1997

Contents

Foreword

Eddie Hammett has always believed deeply in two things. First, he has always believed that a minister of Christian education can achieve world reconciliation as effectively as any other church staff minister. His second deep belief is that the church must learn to be effective as the scattered church in the world.

Many years ago when I was teaching a course entitled "The Renewal of the Church" at the Southern Baptist Theological Seminary, I always emphasized that if renewal were going to be done, the pastor was the one who would have to give the leadership. Eddie, one of the class members, raised his hand and said, "I disagree with you. I think it could be done better by the minister of education." I disagreed with him, emphasizing that the pastor was the one who, through his (at the time I did not say his or her) preaching, would have the greatest opportunity. Eddie and I had a somewhat heated discussion for a number of minutes. Finally he said, "I disagree with your position, and when I graduate from here (if I do), I'm going to prove that you are wrong." When he graduated and went to serve in his first church, he did, indeed, prove that I was wrong. Through the years since then, Eddie and I have kept the closest of personal relationships, and through the years he has continued to prove that I was wrong.

This volume is evidence that he has never lost his interest in and commitment to the renewal of the church. Throughout his ministry, he has been committed to church members and nonchurch members alike, individually and in small groups. Indeed, in the confessions of the unchurched and throughout the book, he cites individuals and couples with whom he has been related.

In the first section of this book, "Is the Church Working?" Hammett gives a general analysis of the problems confronting present-day churches. The culture has so invaded the lives of church members that in the workaday world it is often difficult to see any difference between a church member and a nonchurch member. In this type of culture the only thing that will prepare the church to be a meaningful witness in the next century is a deep and meaningful conversion experience, one that will bring about a radical change in the everyday lives of the present church members.

This is not to say that recent trends toward church growth is inherently wrong. But typically, pastors and staff members who focus only upon church growth emphasize having enough members to build and pay for new buildings, which they insist is a sign of God's blessing. But the size of a church says nothing about how the members live in the world during the week. Perceptive church leaders have known for years that there is something seriously wrong with the present church. The current church stands in need of a radical, authentic conversion experience as the church moves into the 21st century. As Hammett says, "The secularization of our culture is evidence that the church is in need of conversion."

In the second section of the book, "Why the Church Isn't Working," Eddie acknowledges the new religious movements in our society, such as New Age belief and Eastern mysticism. These "religions" are being taken very seriously by a significant number of people. Yet, while these movements attract numbers of people seeking to find some meaning for existence, too often churches seem to be preoccupied with building buildings, raising budgets, and planning programs. In the midst of all of this, churches seem to focus on "churchianity" rather than on Christianity. The church of the next century must take risks and find ways to penetrate the hurting world rather than pamper the present institutional church.

The church of the 21st century must also address the problem of finding volunteer leaders. It is always difficult to get members to serve on the nominating committee. It is even more difficult for the nominating committee to find a sufficient number of people who will accept the responsibility of a leadership position. Unfortunately, very few churches have led their members to discover their spiritual gift(s); nor have they taught them how and where to express their ministry in light of these gifts. A part of the conversion that needs to take place in churches is related to what churches have or have not done concerning the matters of spiritual gifts and ministry.

In the third section of his book, "Making the Church of Today Work," Hammett summarizes the major problems facing the church of today as it approaches the challenges of the next century. Specifically, Hammett deals with two central questions for which today's church must seek biblical answers: (1) What does the church mean by "effectiveness" as it seeks to lead its members to live as Christians in tomorrow's world? (2) What do the leaders of the church mean by "individual conversion" as people "come forward" seeking membership in the church?

The changing roles of what it means to be "family" is one of many issues the church must address if it is to improve its effectiveness. For example, in the 1960s and 1970s, our society understood clearly what it meant to be a family. Family consisted of the married male and female, their children, and their parents and grandparents. But in our culture today we are redefining what it means to be a family. The traditional family continues to exist, but family also includes a male and female who live together without the benefit of marriage, two persons of the same sex who live together with or without the benefit of marriage, those with the dread disease of AIDS who live together, married or unmarried persons of different racial backgrounds who live together, and so on.

"Making the Church of Tomorrow Work" is the title of the fourth section. Here the author gives practical tips to help lead the church from what it is now to what it should be. He explores the shifts and conversions from program development to faith formation, from church focus to world focus, from success to effectiveness, and from the gathered church to the scattered church.

In the fifth section, "Converting the Church for the 21st Century," the author helps Christian leaders see the need for "new wineskins"—to see more clearly the challenge and impact of future trends. He also paints a hopeful and exciting picture of the future church.

This book deals with a serious study of one of the most important issues facing all churches of every denomination. We desperately need to find ways to help churches discover ways of following the teaching of our Lord as recorded in Matthew 28:19-20, "Go therefore and make disciples of all nations, . . . teaching them to obey everything that I have commanded you."

Findley B. Edge

Acknowledgments

I am thankful to many people for the way they have touched my life and this manuscript. Louvenia and Findley Edge are dear friends, always caring and nurturing the vision they planted in me during my seminary days. Their nurture, love, and counsel provided motivation and guidance for this project.

My life and ministry have been deeply touched and blessed by a small group of persons who have not only read and reread this manuscript, but who are integral parts of my learning as expressed here. John Mark and Carla Batchelor are fellow strugglers, pastoral voices, and faithful friends. Jonathan Crawley not only has a keen editing eye but a nurturing and sensitive heart for God. His journey and honest struggle with faith and life have taught me much. Connie Taylor offers constant illustration of a Christian leader at work in the world. Her model and faithfulness inform these writings. William Clemmons has nurtured dreams and guided struggles over the years. For his care and guidance I'll always be grateful.

Co-workers in ministry are frequently sources of encouragement and direction. Thus the writers, speakers, and friendships reflected here are deeply appreciated. Those Christian leaders over the years who have invited me into their struggle of faith and work have been used by God in my life in many ways. The relationships with the unchurched and the dissatisfied are also sources of insight and challenge for which I am grateful.

Finally, I express appreciation to the staff of Smyth & Helwys for asking me to write this book and the excellent editorial work done by Jackie Riley. Their insight, skills, and reliable assistance made this project a joy.

Is the Church Working?

Confessions of the Unchurched

Randy, an unchurched professing Christian, declares, "The church is too judgmental, too negative, too self-serving, and irrelevant for me." This twenty-eight-year-old has found little or no help in the church and is now searching for answers in *The Celestine Prophesy*, Earl Nightengale seminars, and various New Age retreats and workshops. While he finds some help in each of these areas of instruction, his heart is still searching.

David, an active church member, family man, and religious leader, explains during a lengthy conversation, "The church doesn't offer me the community I need to struggle with the real issues in my life." Through fellowship with a small group of fellow strugglers, David discovered God at work. All group members are faithful church people but have found little or no relevant help for life needs in their respective congregations.

Tom and Lisa, a couple from the boomer generation, have a two-year-old daughter. Both are PK's (preacher's kids) who know the good and the bad of the local church. Now they find themselves, after seven years of a deteriorating marriage, facing possible divorce. Can you imagine the pressure on them and their families? They were involved in a church but were not finding help for their hurts nor answers for their questions in traditional programming. The couple separated. Tom came to me for counseling. We started regular dialogues and experiences of spiritual direction. His comment rings in my heart to this day: "The church doesn't want to get its hands dirty, working with persons like me."

Craig, a sincere young man seeking to make peace with his fragmented and stress-filled past, is another unchurched American. His youth, filled with loving parents, church attendance, and security, evolved into times of emotional insecurity and a plummeting self-esteem. This led him to ask hard questions about the church and God. The church could not handle the questions, and God seemed far away. Craig's search for answers had taken him into many unhealthy codependent relationships. His unhealthy behavior and intense search for intimacy left him with HIV and yet another set of issues negatively impacting his self-esteem and self-image. The church had no place for him or his search. Craig's questions needed hearing so that he could reexperience the incarnational love of God through healthy relationships. A small group took on this role when the institutional church left him floundering.

Brian, a professionally trained minister, is active in church leadership but is searching for meaning, hope, and help with the pains and struggles in his own life. His church enjoyed receiving his excellent leadership but did not offer him nor his family a "safe place" to struggle with some difficult issues such as suicide, marital struggles, personal insecurities, homosexuality, alcoholism, and abuse.

Verna, an inquisitive and sincere senior adult, searching for relief from life's struggles, looks to spirituality for answers. The church where she is a member seems to offer no path of resolution for her anger, confusion, and fear. Consequently, she has been inactive for years, although her spiritual quest continues.

For Reflection:

1. Who are the unchurched or the skeptical in your circle of contacts?
2. What have you heard them say, verbally or nonverbally?
3. What insight does this bring to you and/or your church?

An Institution in Trouble

The traditional institutional church is in trouble. It has become more introverted than focused on reaching the world. It is complacent and clergy-directed. In most major denominations membership is down. Denominational and church loyalty is waning. Tithes and offerings are declining and being dispersed to many parachurch organizations. Biblical illiteracy is rampant, even among those who have been actively involved in church life for years.[1] The ills of society are increasing with depth. Seriousness and intensity across all social classes and racial groups are permeating the lives and families of those both inside and outside the church.

Researchers tell us that non-Christians and Christians are basically the same in terms of morality and ethics. Both attend church less and less as the years pass. They declare the church is irrelevant, too judgmental, non-user-friendly, and not worth their time. They are disenchanted with the institutional church. Yet, they are asking serious questions about spiritual issues. They are seeking answers to probing, heartfelt, and challenging questions in every place but the church. The New Age movement, self-help books, motivation seminars, work and civic relationships—you name it! The search goes on, the questions continue to grow, and the church becomes more ineffective.

For Reflection:

Check each statement that applies to your church:

___More money is spent on outreach than on inreach.

___More programming/ministry is aimed at those outside the church than inside.

___Leadership focus is directed toward laypersons rather than toward professaional ministers.

___Membership, attendance, and involvement have increased over the past ten years.

___Members are committed to the beliefs and work of the denomination.

___Tithes and offerings have increased over the past ten years.

___Members are knowledgeable of the Scriptures and doctrine.

___Programming/ministry addresses social problems.

___Different social, economic, and racial groups are represented.

___Members are as concerned about morality and ethics as they were ten years ago.

___Programming/ministry meets the needs of persons in the community as a whole.

___ Types of programming/ministry have changed significantly over the past ten years.

___Members actively share their faith in their daily lives and activities.

What do your answers reveal about your church?

The Need for Conversion

Why are churchgoers and nonchurchgoers alike turning from the traditional model of church to other arenas of spiritual formation? The traditional model of church has lost touch not only with its mission and the culture of which it is a part, but also with its available resources. Certainly, the church is helping some persons to find fellowship, solace, and comfort, but if the church is to impact the world for the cause of Christ, its mission is under serious attack. The church is in need of conversion if it is to regain loyalty, relevancy, and effectiveness in the 21st century. What can be done? Who should tackle the assigment? What will be involved in converting the church? What will a converted church look like?

The need for conversion of the church follows the church renewal movement in the 1960s and 1970s and the church transformation movement in the 1980s and 1990s. Findley Edge, Elton Trueblood, and Keith Miller have written extensively in the area of church renewal. Gordon and Mary Cosby, Robert Schuller, and Elizabeth O'Connor are leaders in the transformation movement. All are in search of the converted church.

Gordon and Mary Cosby share with us these principles of church renewal:

- The church needs to be in the world.
- The shape of the church needs to be shaped to the world's needs.
- The church needs ad hoc structures with the reality that every structure is provisional.
- The church is to be a servant people and not just a people of servant acts.[2]

Currently, they are discussing principles of the transformative church that they believe will impact the 21st century. These principles include:

- A lifelong connectedness with the transformative person and event that would include knowing Jesus and deepening our life of prayer
- A lifelong opposition to the systems under which our lives are bound in our world and nation

7

•A lifelong participation in Jesus' alternative community—the church[3]

Findley Edge offers the church challenges that help insure biblical integrity, offer practical applications, and pull us into the 21st century. Insights include:

•All Christians are called, gifted, and sent into ministry.
•The priesthood of all believers is a pathway for activating Christian faith in the church, family, society, and world.[4]
•Regenerative church membership is necessary in carrying out God's mission in the church and in the world.
•Formative and reformative church discipline are critical to insure effectiveness and growth of God's people.[5]
•Christian education and spiritual formation are modeled and taught within the community of faith and should have specific goals and an intent for life change.[6]

Elton Trueblood, a teacher-mentor-friend to Edge and the Cosbys, offers what are still fresh challenges for the church as we move into the next century:

•The development and nurture of the Christian faith grows best in the context of small groups/community.
•The work of the church is not only the responsibility of all the people of God (both clergy and laity), but must also happen in the "gathered church" and the "scattered church."[7]

These innovators in the faith, along with many others, are our prophetic voices during these days of wilderness journey for the church as we struggle to maintain biblical integrity, relational authenticity, and cultural sensitivity. Our challenge now is to find ways to impact and transform the unchurched, secularized culture in which we find ourselves.

The first step of this conversion should involve self-examination, evaluation, and revisitation of our loyalties to Christ. Bill Hull summarizes the church's dilemma in *Building High Commitment in a Low-Commitment World*. He says,

The enemy that keeps the church from reaping a great harvest comes from within. Attempts to make it more relevant and user-friendly at the expense of its discipline and health seriously weaken the church. On top of this, moral relativism and materialism have gradually seduced the church, shredding its integrity [8]

Claims of both researchers and unchurched persons and the clear biblical mandate to "go and make disciples" call the church to conversion if it is to survive and be effective in ministry in the 21st century. We as individual Christians must spend time and energy reaffirming our individual conversion experiences and challenging the corporate body toward conversion. We must change from what is unhealthy, sinful, and wayward to what is healthy, godly, and focused on following Christ.

For Reflection:

1. How do you react to the thesis that the church is in need of conversion?
2. What indicators of the need for conversion do you feel are applicable to individuals?

Conclusion

During my twenty-plus years of professional ministry in local churches, denominational seminaries, and state conventions I've found significant guidance, help, and hope in the ministry of the local church. In the last ten years or so, however, I've encountered a growing number of persons with a thirst for God but a distrust for and disapproval of the ministry of the local church.

Such experiences and relationships have caused me to struggle with issues raised in this volume. God has blessed this struggle and allowed me to catch a glimpse of some new methods to relate the life-changing message of the gospel in this skeptical pluralistic generation. This book is a vehicle for dialogue and reflection for clergy and laypersons who, like me, are concerned about the growing ineffectiveness of the institutional church in our pluralistic secular culture.

This text will allow you individually and collectively to reexamine your walk with Christ and the mission of the church you are committed to follow. Every issue raised has a library of books written about it, but I hope this overview will allow time and opportunity to reflect on being an effective Christian in the 21st century and developing a pathway toward that effectiveness. Let's struggle together to identify conversions the church must experience if we are to be effective in the new century.

For Reflection:

1. What issues and questions have surfaced thus far in your reading?
2. Review the quotes by other writers cited in this section. Which seems to summarize your feeling best? Why?

Notes

[1]George Barna, *Biblical Recorder*, 28 September 1996, 9; *Western Recorder*, 17 September 1996, 8. (Seven out of ten adults say religious faith is very important in their lives today. They have not assumed that Christianity is the starting point for their search.)

[2]Presentation by Mary Cosby, the Edge Festival, Southern Baptist Theological Seminary, Louisville KY, 27-29 October 1986.

[3]Presentation by Mary Cosby, Cooperative Baptist Fellowship, Richmond VA, June 1996.

[4]Additional information found in Findley B. Edge, *The Greening of the Church* (Atlanta: Home Mission Board, 1986) and Findley B. Edge, *The Doctrine of the Laity* (Nashville: Convention Press, 1985).

[5]See Findley B. Edge, *Quest for Vitality in Religion* (Macon GA: Smyth & Helwys, 1995).

[6]See Findley B. Edge, *Teaching for Results* (Nashville: Broadman Press, 1995)

[7]See Elton Trueblood, *The Incendiary Fellowship* (New York: Harper & Row, 1967) and *Company of the Committed* (San Francisco: Harper & Row, 1961).

[8]Bill Hull, *Building High Commitment in a Low-Commitment World* (Ventura CA: Regal Publishers, 1996) 8.

Why the Church
Isn't Working

The Unchurched Culture

Christians are called to be "salt, light, and leaven." The function of salt is to season and preserve. The presence of light pushes back the darkness and illuminates the good. Leaven, when worked into the dough, permeates and impacts the whole loaf. Our presence as Christians is, by God's design, to impact the world for God's purposes. Yet, the salt seems to have "lost its savor." Salt applies to the church as well as to the individual Christian. When the church strays from its intended function, not only does the church lose, but the surrounding culture also loses. It no longer has light, hope, and the values of the Christian community that the church provides. Until the church renews its vows to Christ as an agent of redemption and reconciliation and as a peacemaker, the culture will penetrate and drive the church. Many have said that the church is looking and acting more like the world and that it is increasingly difficult to tell the churched from the unchurched. A 1996 Gallup study summarizes this trend best by declaring, "One of the seeming paradoxes of American society is that religion is gaining ground, but morality is losing ground."[1]

When the Christian community has no distinctiveness from the non-Christian world, the church is in trouble, and the world is in trouble. A major part of the mission of the church is to impact the culture with the message of Jesus Christ. We are to be his representatives in the world and allow his light to shine in and through us in our daily lives. Yet, too often it seems that the mission and message of Christ have been overshadowed if not overpowered by the cultural messages and mission, thus weakening or losing the church's value and distinctiveness in the world.

Crime, violence, victimization, poverty, injustices, racism, bigotry, hatred, pride, winning at all cost, and other realities are indicative of our secular state. Has the church in any way been responsible for this shift in values? Why have these secular values seemed to overtake and overshadow the values of the Christian church? When such secularization occurs, what is the impact on the church and the Christian community? The following evidences of secularization point toward the church's need of conversion.

(1) *The church has lost its influence.* Christian values are being replaced by or overshadowed by the secular values of our culture.

The 1996 Gallup poll revealed that "Americans' depth of commitment to religious faith is less impressive than their attachment to organized religion."[2] Rarely do you hear of the church impacting the world. Granted there may be some indirect influence, but a proactive, intentional-focused influence toward the church's need for conversion has been waning over the last several decades. We must examine the many arenas of need in our world: hunger, hurting people, joblessness, poverty, injustice. Where is the church's voice and action in advocacy issues, abuse issues, immorality issues, issues of injustice to all age and people groups, joblessness, poverty, and injustice? Often we hear the church's voice of judgment or ridicule, but the culture misses the actions of redemption, healing, and refocusing of society around Christian teachings and values.

(2) *Success standards are confused.* In the educational system and the medical, legal, and business worlds, our standards are more in line with the capitalistic system than with the call of servanthood and self-giving. The church has taken a backseat in formulating standards and values in many segments of society. Why do each of these systems cry for help and guidance, but Christians in these respective systems rarely take a serious step toward helping change the system? Instead of Christians shaping the system, the system shapes them.

(3) *Spirituality is rampant in society but weak, if not void, in the church.* The New Age movement, Eastern mysticism, and the conservative movement in our culture—to name a few—have nurtured the thirst for spirituality and meaning-making in our society. At the same time, the church seems to have become more preoccupied with buildings, budgets, and programming than with intentionally nurturing people in the faith and working with the issues of inner life, spirituality, and meaning-making. It almost seems that the church is busy answering questions no one is asking. The church has become so institutionalized that it has fossilized its potential for effectiveness in the secular culture.

(4) *Christian values are frequently overshadowed by cynics and skeptics who challenge us to be consistent in our walk and talk.* Christianity and religion have taken such a beating in the media over the last decade that the skeptics and often the religious find

16

it difficult to trust the message and ministry of today's Christian community.

(5) *Secular culture has permeated every phase of life with its message and mission.* Meanwhile, Christianity has continued to give primary emphasis to institutional models. Christianity has not created new and varied delivery systems for the message or the mission. The institutionalization of the church might be the greatest barrier the Christian message has in this secular, unchurched culture.[3]

Cultural trends and the pressures of society have already forced the church to make several shifts in an effort to become acceptable and relevant to today's youth and adults. For instance, we hear much about becoming a "user-friendly church" or a "seeker-sensitive congregation." Thirty to forty-five-minute sermon monologues have been replaced by visual and dramatic simulations about life issues and guided by biblical narratives. Some churches have sacrificed the hymnody of tradition for the upbeat music and catchy lyrics of contemporary society. Others might say that lock-ins, ski trips, and fun-filled retreat settings for youth, college students, and young adults are the results of the culture impacting the church. Still others would suggest that taking senior adults on trips, cruises, and leisure excursions are illustrative of culture's impact.

We may question if the early church was similarly impacted by the culture. Did the early church have the same structures and traditions as our fathers and mothers? Did the early church impact its culture, or did the culture impact the early church? When is it appropriate for the culture to impact the nature of the church, and when should the church impact the culture?

Culture infiltrating and driving the nature of the church is one thing, but cultural shifts changing the mission of the church is quite another thing! The gospel must be communicated in ways the current age can understand and respond to, but the message of the gospel must never be diminished so that it is more acceptable or palatable for the culture in which it seeks to speak and direct. When culture rather than conviction to Christian principles and values begins to guide a church, the church is in need of conversion. Otherwise, the church will inevitably drift into maintenance rather than move forward in mission.

For Reflection:

1. When the economic crunch or the summer slump hits your church, where do you look for answers—secular issues or spiritual concerns?

2. When you decide to make changes in programming or scheduling, what drives the decision—culture or spiritual issues?

3. When the church is in trouble due to a decline or controversy, what roots of the problem are quickly identified—leadership concerns or spiritual concerns?

4. When the church is not impacting the community for Christ, what reasons are quickly identified—secular issues/problems or spiritual concerns/problems?

The Emerging Leadership Void

Over the last fifteen to twenty years, there has been a growing consensus and clarity that the training of most clergy is out-of-date prior to their graduation from seminary. It is also clear that most professional clergy and most denominations have little or no required continuing education built into their ministry goals. How can those who are trained to lead the congregation, but are ill-equipped themselves, be found fruitful, relevant, and effective in a culture and generation that is filled with professionals who are victims of career downsizing and refunctioning? How can leaders be effective in leading when the followers are far ahead of most of the leaders in technological understanding, cultural sensitivity, time management, refunctioning and reengineering, as well as total quality management issues?

Lay leaders in churches are undertrained also. In most situations, the church seeks leaders without supplying them proper equipment, curricula, or training. The church often finds itself with committee members who are part of meetings with no agenda and who spin their wheels without being effective. As a result, these committee members become discouraged, under-challenged, and ill-tempered toward irrelevant curricula and meetings.

What can be done with this reality and ongoing tension? Leaders must be converted from their agendas to God's agenda, from out-of-date training to effective and relevant training, from "churchianity" to Christianity, and from a program orientation to a mission/ministry orientation. Both clergy and laity must be involved in ongoing relevant continuing education, mentoring, and accountability relationships that help maintain focus and relevancy. Clusters of churches need to work together on troubling issues. The issues of today are so complex, local, and fluid that ongoing multidisciplinary reflection and exploration are vital to effective and efficient decision making and leadership in the 21st century. Leaders must be risk takers and move beyond the familiar, comfortable, and secure to what is unknown. We need to move the church toward its calling, to what is relevant and penetrates the hurting world rather than to what nurtures and coddles the institutional church.

Leaders must have persons following them, though not necessarily the masses. Consider the example of Jesus. He had only a remnant of persons he actually led, and some of them not only resisted his counsel but often veered from his course. However, many followed him from village to village seeking, searching, and wanting to listen, waiting to see him do miracles no one else could do, asking him for healing for the hurting.

Leaders are difficult to find, at least by the methods we traditionally use to discover leaders. Most churches seek leaders through a nominating committee process, a committee on committee process, by word of mouth from others, or by family affiliation. We have a leadership void because our definition and methodology of discovering and utilizing leaders are limited at best. We must seek to involve people in the actual mission of the church rather than just to enlist leaders to staff a program. We must identify, equip, and recognize leaders through various other means. Some avenues of discovering effective Christian leaders are:

- relationships
- new member orientation
- mentoring relationships and apprenticeships
- listening to the burdens and dreams of others
- challenging persons to follow their dreams
- creating new channels for leading and ministry

Because our leadership base is limited by our vision and definition of leadership, the church is not reaping the full benefit of the leaders God has already placed within the body of Christ. I firmly believe that God has given the church all the leaders it needs to do all the work of the local congregation (1 Cor 12). The problem is often explained away by saying, "If our people were more committed, we could do more." While there may be some truth to this, I would suggest that our commitment levels are low and our leadership base is limited because our methods and channels of leadership and ministry are too traditional, too institutionally tied, and not relevant enough for the times in which we live. The burdens, visions, dreams, and challenges of church leaders go far beyond being good Sunday School teachers, or building committee members, or deacons.

Some leaders want to find and join God working in the public school system that is filled with fear due to violence, drugs, and consequences of broken and blended families. Other leaders are concerned about the homeless—being their advocate, their care-givers, their tutors. Still others are burdened with and in the midst of helping persons struggling with family crises such as death, divorce, financial distress, loss of jobs, and health. What would happen if those with the burden for a particular area of human hurt and need were encouraged to lead the congregation —at least those in the congregation with similar interests. I believe that they would find strength and guidance and excite-ment in studying Scripture together, exploring God's plan together, and working together as disciples. Consider the following:

•Suzanne, a public school algebra teacher, decided to build rela-tionships with her students and their families who shared their personal struggles with her. She meets with them voluntarily outside the classroom and has been found to "bear much fruit" by helping to heal fractured relationships, referring the disillu-sioned to counselors, and leading persons to Christ.

•Ron, a manager of a chain of restaurants, sees himself as the pastor of all his employees. He prays for and with them. He nur-tures them and theirs during their stressful days and offers spiritual care and guidance when needed.

•David, an attorney, has found great fulfillment and personal ministry as an advocate for the poor in the politics of the inner city. He rallies church members and community leaders to rebuild the inner city dwellings and provides support for the poor.

Christian leaders in the 21st century must be more tied to Christ's mission in the world of brokenness than to the institu-tional concerns of the local congregation. We are called to "be" the church, rather than to build the church. The local church base is needed for effective ministry, mission, and maturity in Christ, but the local church base must not be the focus of ministry and mission, lest we miss the Great Commission. Such a shift will be a major conversion for Christian leaders and particularly those who lead in the church. We have spent so much of our energy, time, and money leading inside the church to create a safe haven for Christians or a place of corporate education and worship, we have almost ignored being Christian leaders in the world.

Leaders will be challenged to lead to places the body of Christ has yet to explore. The unchurched culture will challenge leaders to learn to minister to the unlovely, to those who have little or no appreciation or understanding of our church language. In fact, the unchurched will probably not learn our church language. We will have to learn theirs in order to communicate in ways that will introduce them to the Good News and ultimately lead them to Christ and his church. We are already seeing seeker-sensitive churches utilizing drama, media, movie and television clips, radio spots, and Internet web sites in their ministry. There are "Fax of Life" distributed to local Christian business people as well as committee meetings and task force meetings on the web, reaching members all over the world. Such attempts to speak to and from the familiar secular world with sacred truths are steps in the right direction.

For Reflection:

1. Who are the remnant people in your congregation or circle of influence?
2. Who are the Christian leaders you can identify who have ministries in the workplace?
3. Summarize your understanding of "being the church."

Changing Family Issues

Church, as we have known it, has been mostly focused on, comfortable with, and challenged by the traditional family structure of the 1950s and 1960s. The challenge of the church both now and in the future will be finding ways to minister to, reach, evangelize, teach, and resource the nontraditional family of the 21st century.

Family is being redefined in our society to include clusters of persons both married and unmarried who live together, persons of biological connections, and many others with relational connections, who have become surrogate families in our mobile society. Economic conditions are forcing adults of all ages to live together as well as share expenses, housing, and parenting responsibilities. Diversity, human rights, and our increasingly pluralistic society are confronting the church with interracial relationships and marriages; biracial children and adults; homosexual relationships; sequential monogamous relationships; blended families; and different parenting styles, communication patterns, and family traditions. Yes, today and tomorrow, family is being defined differently, from persons with AIDS who live together for support or care to senior adults who live together due to economic limitations, and all are calling themselves family.

In addition, careers are moving into homes. Job sharing and downsizing are creating flex schedules that often bring less time for family interaction than most would desire. Family communication, when attempted, is through E-mail or video or audio messages rather than face-to-face conversations. Such career issues are certain to create new challenges and opportunities for the family and the church.

Technology is another challenge to family and social issues. From electronic mail to euthanasia, from computers to cancer, technology will have its impact. How will the church deal with issues that are being forced by technology, such as life-and-death issues, making decisions about the quality and quantity of life, doctor-assisted suicide, insurance and medical costs, and an increasing number of aging adults?

Ministry to families must be broadened to include the growing diversity in our society. Many will say that the church must maintain traditional family values and uphold traditional biblical family understanding. While I do believe this is the ideal and

God's desire, I believe even more that God's desire is "to bring good news to the oppressed, to bind up the brokenhearted, to proclaim liberty to the captives, and release to the prisoners" (Isa 61:1). If the church limits its ministry only to the traditional family models, it is missing a vitally important arena for ministry as well as a growing number of our population. God calls us to preserve Christian values, but God also calls us to "go into the roads and lanes and compel people" (Luke 14:23). God calls us to follow the model of Christ as he related to the Samaritan woman, Nicodemus, the lepers, and the sinful. Scripture reminds us repeatedly about Christ's fellowship with the sinners as well as his noncondemning attitude toward sinners. He consistently calls us to "love one another," "forgive one another," and "go into all the world" with the Good News.

The converted church must acknowledge and struggle with how to effectively minister to the families of our age. How do we communicate the Good News in these new relationships? How can we validate and communicate with the persons who are in non-Christian relationships without isolating them from moving toward Christ and his love? How can we build trustworthy relationships with families inside and outside the church walls so that biblical truths might be modeled and/or taught? Let me make a few suggestions.

(I) *Pay attention to language.* Phrases in church bulletins, conversations, and prayers that limit the definition of family to traditional lines often isolate and hurt those who do not feel included.

(2) *Provide networking opportunities.* Those who are in similar life and family situations need opportunities to network, build community among themselves for additional support, and create learning opportunities. This networking may be through retreats, seminars, support groups, classes, fellowships, or something as sophisticated as a web page or a newsletter for a given target group.

(3) *Plan and schedule events and experiences that have clear purposes.* When planning for Christian education, understand that in an unchurched culture we must do pre-Christian education for unchurched persons. For instance, what about an unchurched, unmarried couple who approaches the church to

dedicate their newborn during the parent/child dedication service? The traditional church might frown upon this because the
couple is not married, when instead the open congregation might
use this as a teaching/learning opportunity for the couple and the
congregation. Some customizing of the event would be important
and valuable in their pre-Christian journeys as they grow into the
"in Christ" relationship. The journey from "in and of the world"
to "being in Christ" is a long trip for many, but every long
journey begins with the first step.

(4) *Value the people groups for what they provide.* There are
many biblical illustrations of these various family configurations
that could be ways of nurturing, informing and/or validating
these relationships, and providing forums for growth and development. Blended families, interracial relationships, families in
various types of distress, unwed mothers, absent fathers, and
unchurched persons seeking help and healing and hope are all
part of our Scriptures. You might need to take an inventory of the
families in the church and community. (See the Needs Assessment in the appendix.) Who are they? Where are they? What are
their needs as they perceive them? What are their needs as you
perceive them? What bridge-building experiences might you facilitate to move them toward Christ? Discover these persons. Teach
them, and let them teach us!

For Reflection:

1. What types of families are in your church's sphere of
influence?
2. In light of current and future family trends, how does your
church minister effectively in this new day and age?
3. What are the concerns and stumbling blocks for you and/or
your church in ministering to the new families of this day and
age?
4. What steps can be taken to help refine and improve your
ministry to families with the issues and hurts they encounter?
5. What type of church life schedule can best accommodate new
family and career challenges?
6. Where will church leaders be focused in this change?
7. What type of worship and Christian education will be needed?

Lack of Community

With the diversity and mobility in our culture, dysfunctional family systems, and the isolation in our society, churches must design intentional strategies to help people experience a sense of community. We must help those who join the church to feel as though they belong in the church family. Many join but do not feel they belong to our churches, while others do not join because they see no way to belong to our tightly formed "holy huddles." There are varied reasons for this failure to become involved in the church community.

Loneliness is a national disease that creeps in upon persons of every age and culture as a result of our busyness, fears, mobility, and dysfunction. How can the church help persons overcome loneliness as together we learn to build and grow from community?

Isolationism is rampant among all ages and includes those who are isolated because of family distress, dysfunctional behaviors, varying cultural backgrounds, or workaholics searching for some respite and relief. Others experiencing a double dose of isolationism include the aged who are warehoused in nursing homes and those with AIDS. How can the church help these persons to move beyond isolationism to community?

Cocooning seems to be characteristic of the boomers and busters, working hard and coming home and "cocooning" until another workday. They do not want to leave the warmth and safety of home for any reason. Their entertainment, socializing, and dining occur within the safety and security of the cocoon. How can the church teach, disciple, nurture, and build community with those who are bent toward living this way?

The church is increasingly challenged to address these and other sociological phenomena as it pursues effective ministry in the 21st century. While each phenomenon has much to say to the church in need of conversion, it also creates the reality of the need for intentional community building. How can the church effectively reach persons who are from these and other trends of family, culture, and society?

The Christian church must find and feel the burden of learning to enfold those from our new culture who are needing or seeking a place in the church and/or Christian faith. The

Scriptures call us to be a community of faith, a family, the body of Christ, and the bridegroom of Christ, all of which are relational phrases that point to the vitally important role of relationships in the Christian faith. We will be effective in reaching others only to the degree that we are effective and intentional about developing relationships.

In years gone by, the church focused on developing and maintaining programs, but now we must focus on developing and maintaining relationships. It does not just happen after one gathering or an introduction. It is built over time through consistency, intentionality, and friendship. Following are some suggestions about enfolding persons into the life of the church and the Christian faith that might be helpful in our unchurched, seeker-oriented culture.

- Share coffee breaks and lunch in the workplace.
- Invite newcomers in the community to share coffee or be part of a backyard community barbecue.
- Create clusters of families and family members who have similar interests or responsibilities (for example, live in the same community, work in the same areas, attend the same schools, share similar hobbies/interests).
- Create opportunities for persons to form support groups around similar struggles and hurts.
- Network persons via Internet, E-mail, and bulletin boards.
- Provide groupings around common needs/stages of life (for example, blended families, divorce recovery, single parents, empty nesters, transplants).
- Host new member banquets, receptions, and retreats.
- Build community among newcomers rather than trying only to enfold newcomers into the existing congregation.
- Provide intentional new member orientation/training seminars that build community, instruct about church life, and create other open doors and possibilities for personal growth and developing other relationships.
- Create mentoring/apprenticeship relationships among those in the existing church and those who are seeking to belong and grow (for example, among church leaders, community leaders, business leaders, and families).

Relationship is vital to a person's spiritual and social growth and also to closing the back-door syndrome of churches while strengthening the front-door ministry of churches. That is, many churches lose members who have not connected with someone personally within the first six weeks of their membership. With a system and set of relationships that help people know and feel they belong and are cared for as a vital part of the community, church membership statistics could reflect more consistency, less back-door losses, and more persons wanting to join and belong.

In a pluralistic, diverse, and unchurched culture we must begin our discipling and community building prior to church membership or conversion. We must prove our value and trustworthiness through our initiative, consistency, and faithfulness in and through preconversion and premembership strategies. This is a major shift of our energies, priorities, and resources. The first step toward membership and conversion for newcomers to a community may not be a church event, but rather a community-wide event that is nonthreatening and focuses on building relationships that in turn provide another step toward friendship, Christian faith, membership, and church involvement.

Another shift is to open appropriate leadership opportunities to non-Christian nonmembers, thus allowing them to contribute their skills to the church's ministry even before conversion as a way of enfolding them into the life of the congregation. Examples might include participating in the music program, or coaching, or co-leading sports teams or task force groups. In doing this, they might continue to explore Christian beliefs and practices. This is quite a shift for some churches and must be encouraged and modeled by progressive church leaders who understand the unique features of our unchurched culture.

For Reflection:

1. What are the implications of this section for you? For your congregation?
2. How are you emotionally responding to the challenge presented here? Why?
3. What might be the end result if you incorporated these insights into your personal and church life?

Failure to Walk the Talk

In an unchurched culture everyone seems to be looking for faults in the church. Television evangelists, church staff members who have fallen to sexual temptations, and church leaders who are inconsistent in their Christian witness as a church leader on Sunday to an unethical tyrant on Monday in the workplace are fueling the skeptical world's distrust of the church. In recent days the media has captured on film the struggle in some denominations over homosexuality, ordination, and unethical practices of religious leaders. In my own denomination we have spent more than ten years fighting among ourselves, which fuels the world's disdain for the life and ministry of the church in today's world. Survey after survey reveals that many feel the church of today is irrelevant and noneffective in dealing with the issues, as well as inconsistent in its walk and talk. Such criticisms are probably more true than false and should serve to awaken Christian leaders to the need for being honest about our humanity and brokenness, rather than continuing to set ourselves up as untouchable or as religious icons.

We need to learn to be honest about our frailty, humanity, and brokenness. We need to confess to the world and to each other that we are lost in a new unchurched world, clamoring for the love, attention, and respect we have known in years gone by. We must confess that in many ways what we are doing in and through the church is not working. We continue to do things the same way we have always done them while expecting different results. We are afraid to let go of what we are familiar with, trained for, and committed to, and search out and follow the Spirit's leading into effective ministry as we move into the 21st century.

Most Christian leaders know that what we are doing falls far short of meeting the multiplicity of needs in our world, but most are without a clue, or the courage, to decide what changes need to be implemented to insure greater effectiveness. We need to confess that in most cases what we argue about, invest in, and train for is perpetuating the institutional church we know and love, the one that has nurtured us, married us, and been inspirational and directional in our lives. We have done this to the exclusion of arguing about, investing in, and training for "doing church" and "being church" in our changing age. We do not have a respectable track record with the homeless, the destitute, and AIDS victims. We avoid dealing with those who live together out of wedlock, those who choose alternative lifestyles, those who are unfaithful in relationships, abusers and victims of abuse, the emotionally immature, the biblically ignorant, and those who are filled with anger about the unjust actions in our world. The list goes on and on amid the silence of the church in unjust times.

Our agendas and meetings are filled with issues related to institutional preservation, job security, and comfort. We are lost with how to rework meetings and agendas around the relevant, pressing issues even though they scream for our attention. A Christian man struggling over a wife's affair, his anger, his love, their child, and his commitment to Christ, once said to me, "The church doesn't want to touch the dirty or tough issues." One can see that this man was in terrible pain, searching deeply into himself and his faith for help and guidance, yet his local church had not been in touch with him in a meaningful and consistent way. Unfortunately, this man's assessment bears much truth. Churches and Christian leaders really do not know how, or have the support and encouragement, to grapple with the tough issues of our age.

Most likely, the church will have to spend a lot of money to find some new answers. It will have to invest in people who may never come to our churches nor contribute to our budgets. We are likely to do ministries and conduct programs that are not concerned about institutional preservation, but rather carry out Christ's command to "love one another as he loved us." In years to come, we most certainly will need to be more concerned about "being" church than building a church. The church of Christ will continue to exist and is God's plan for redeeming the world. However, we need to return to the original purpose for church. The early church was not clergy-driven nor institutionally-bound. Rather, it was Christ-centered, need-driven, community-based, and Spirit-led.

For Reflection:

1. What are your reactions to this section?
2. What are the implications of this thought pattern for Christian leaders and the corporate church?
3. If these concepts were taken seriously, what implications do you see for yourself? Your church? The unchurched? The community? The workplace?

Maintenance vs. Mission

What are the indicators that a church is drifting into maintaining an organization of rituals, traditions, and relationships?

- When committee meetings focus on institutional concerns (budgets, maintenance, and relationships) rather than on mission concerns (reaching new people groups, reconciling relationships, rallying to change the injustices in the community and/or world)
- When budget planning begins with what we have to work with rather than what God has in mind for us
- When annual planning consists of doing what we did last year just on another calendar date or maybe even on the same date one year later
- When most conversations revolve around meeting the needs of those in attendance rather than reaching those who are not in attendance
- When planning, budgeting, and calendaring revolve around institutional buildings and schedules rather than around the needs, conveniences, and comfort zones of those outside the organization
- When preserving programs, traditions, and rituals get more meeting time, dialogue time, and budget than creating and resourcing new strategies to reach the unchurched, lost, and broken world
- When people's intent and energy focus more on humoring those in the pew than on penetrating their communities, families, and workplaces for the cause of Christ

These issues are only representative of specific ones that capture the interest of many churches and distract from fulfilling their mission. A church that turns to maintenance most always has an inward focus rather than an outward focus.

For Reflection:

1. If you used the seven items on the checklist as an evaluation of your church's passions, foci, and budgeting, how many checks would there be?
2. How many checks are representative of your church body?
3. What type of church/Christian are you?

Inward Focus vs. Outward Focus

The last several decades have proven to be a time when many churches have suffered from becoming inwardly focused. When all the world around us is changing at such a rapid pace, many of the baby busters and senior adults who comprise much of the church population have decided to fasten down the hatches and create "a sanctuary"—a safe, comfortable, familiar place. This move has pushed the church to an inward focus and pulled it away from the outward focus mandated by Christ and needed by the world. What indicators suggest an inwardly-focused class, group, or congregation?

- When conversations, meetings, budgets, and leaders focus more on taking care of the members rather than on reaching the unchurched
- When people bask in feelings and situations reflected by one or more of the following phrases:

"We have the greatest fellowship."
"Our class/group is so close."
"We are good at taking care of one another."
"When someone from our class or church is in need, we are there."
"We want to grow, but we're not going to change the way we do things."

- When planning events, experiences, menus, and activities, decisions are made exclusively on what is best for our group or church rather than what might be more effective in reaching new groups of persons
- When personal or institutional needs and history are given priority over needs and concerns of the unchurched or the prospective members
- When conflict erupts because someone inside the church is needing attention, but the same type of conflict and concern do not surface when someone outside the church is needing attention

An inwardly-focused church is a dying and ineffective church since the Great Commission, which describes the mission of the church, is outwardly focused. Yet, many churches seem to be much more inwardly focused than outwardly focused. Such a condition often brings warmth of fellowship to the congregation, but also contributes life-draining, mission-diluting activity that insures certain death and ineffectiveness of fulfilling the biblical mandate to "go into all the world." Years of introversion yield an apathetic church, often filled with dissension or exclusionary membership.

For Reflection:

1. How do you feel about these indicators?
2. Which indicators speak to you personally?
3. Which indicators describe the group, class, or church of which you are a part?
4. Do you know of other indicators you could add to this list?
5. What might be done to help shift an inward focus to an outward focus?

Apathy vs. Activity

How many times have you heard these statements?

"Our church's problem is not the need for adequate programming but the need for leaders to run the programs."
"Our church leaders are just not committed enough."
"Our leaders are so out of touch with the times and needs of our community that our church is fast becoming a mausoleum."

Do you ever hear statements such as these?

"Our leaders are energized and committed to leading the church to fulfill the Great Commission."
"Our leaders are eager to help each other, share responsibilities, and move the church forward in ways that the community has to take note."

Leadership is a, if not *the*, critical issue in most churches and denominations today. Without effective Christian leaders the church is destined to flounder, stand still, and become introverted, self-serving, and ineffective. Unless the leaders catch the vision and activate the needed skills to lead the church toward effectiveness, the world and the church will pay the price. Watch for these signs of apathy in leaders:

• Involved in many meetings but experience few results
• Avoid planning and are usually reactive rather than proactive
• Try to lead by position or status rather than by modeling and vision
• Seek to motivate others by words rather than by vision and plan
• Create aimlessness that turns into anxiety and frustration for themselves and others
• Generate decreasing excitement, involvement, and faithfulness to assigned responsibilities

Which of the above signs are characteristic of your church leadership? Count the number of persons to whom these would apply. If one-third of your church leadership base exhibits most of these characteristics, a leadership development process or change must be made soon. Not addressing these signs of apathy destines individuals, congregations, and the Great Commission to poverty, if not failure. Consider these hints for activating leaders:

• Affirm those who are effective in leadership.
• Provide vision and encouragement for all leaders.
• Discover and utilize spiritual gifts in the leadership development process.
• Check and inspect the things you feel are important in accomplishing church goals and dreams in fulfilling the Great Commission.
• Network like-minded or burdened leaders, and empower them to discern the heart of God and move forward in their ministries.
• Recognize that all are called to ministry and are significant parts of the body of Christ (1 Cor 12; Rom 12:1).
• Create accountability relationships for persons seeking to grow in Christ and in their leadership roles.

Until the Christian community decides to be intentional about developing and empowering Christian leaders to be obedient followers of Christ, we are sabotaging God's design. The church must begin training, ordaining, commissioning, and sending forth Christian leaders so that the church base might remain strong, active, relevant, and alive. But the church must also begin training, ordaining, commissioning, and sending forth Christian leaders into Christian leadership roles within the community, workplace, and world if we are to become actively concerned about the masses.

For Reflection:

1. What would happen if the church commissioned Christian leaders to impact their work world as a valid part of their ministry?
2. What would happen if the church saw its primary ministry as developing leaders to penetrate the world rather than finding leaders to perpetuate a program?

Conclusion

How long has the church of today been ineffective in this culture? How long will we ignore the changes in the world and cling to our traditions that may make us comfortable, but are obviously not relevant or admired by the unchurched world we are supposed to be reaching and evangelizing? How can we be honest with ourselves and the call of Christ to his church without exploring these questions seriously? It seems that the mission of God, or at least our role in it, hinges on our ability to be honest at this point before we can move forward. How long has it been since today's church, which has served us well for part of its history, has been effective in this culture?

For Reflection:

1. How do you feel about what you are reading?
2. Do you want to argue with my observations and conclusions? If so, please summarize them and share them with fellow leaders to check your objectivity and honesty.

Notes

[1]George Gallup, *Emerging Trends*, Princeton Religion Research Center Newsletter, quoted in *Western Recorder*, 5 November 1996, 1.

[2]Marv Knox, *Biblical Recorder*, 5 November 1996, 1.

[3]See George Hunter, *Church for the Unchurched* (Nashville: Cokesbury, 1996); or Walt Kallestad, *Taking the Church Public* (Nashville: Cokesbury, 1996).

Making the Church
of Today Work

Turning Ineffectiveness into Effectiveness

The church today is faced with the same situation as the early church. It must share the gospel in a foreign land, a pagan culture, a world filled with values unlike those of the Christian tradition and faith. How can we reverse the trend of church ineffectiveness in this culture? How can we turn ineffectiveness into effectiveness?

The greatest challenge before church leadership is how to remain true to scripture and effective in reaching and ministering to an unchurched culture. Just as our current and past Christian leaders were trained to interpret the Scriptures, we must learn to interpret our culture as a preparation for planting seeds of the Good News.

Walter Brueggeman, an Old Testament scholar, claims that there are compelling parallels between our contemporary communities of faith and the community of Israel during the time of the exile. He further observes that we are dislocated emotionally and spiritually because we are living in an era in which we have lost many of the privileges, certitudes, and institutions we previously took for granted. He suggests a return to these basics in order to cope with this dislocation.

- Learn to speak and converse about feelings of sadness, loss, and anger.
- Practice "ordered holiness," the discipline of treating persons and things as vehicles of the sacred rather than as mere commodities.
- Engage in imaginative compassion toward neighbors, remembering that neighbors include "the poor, widows, orphans, strangers, and aliens."
- Expect that God will come with the news of newness.[1]

The new church will be a church converted from what worked in yesterday's culture to what will work in the emerging unchurched culture. Yes, the church must undergo a conversion, a change from patterns of our "old life" as we seek to function in "newness." Note some conversions that must occur.

- Conversion needs to be defined more clearly and worked with more intentionally in an unchurched culture.

•A balance is needed between biblical mandates and maintenance passions.
•A converted church must nurture people in conversion, impact culture, produce healthy disciples, be intentional about being and doing church, and redefine success/effectiveness.

These challenges come from reflecting on indicators and manifestations of our ineffectiveness. If we have been ineffective in some areas, what will make us effective? Read on for insights about effectiveness in an unchurched culture as well as suggestions on conversions the church will likely be confronted with as it moves toward greater effectiveness. The four insights prompting conversion are:

•Moving from program development to faith formation
•Moving from a church focus to a world focus
•Moving from success to effectiveness
•Moving from a "gathered church" model to a "scattered church" orientation

For Reflection:

1. Do you agree that the institutional church needs to be converted to become more effective in the 21st century?
2. How do you respond to the conversions suggested?

Mirroring God's Realities

So the church is in need of conversion. But how can the church experience conversion while moving full steam ahead with weekly services, church staff, church programs, formal and informal leaders, traditions, church politics, denominational ties, community functions, and so on? It is not realistic, in most situations, to stop everything and start a converted mission-oriented congregation, but several realistic steps can be pursued that will facilitate conversion and help the church move forward in God's mission.

When speaking of the church, we must not lose sight of scriptural teachings about conversion. After all, the church really is people. God is calling people to be on mission, under divine power. The church of today often gets this mission tangled with its desires, agendas, and purposes. In fact, frequently church leaders wrestle over personal agendas more than over God's desires. Somehow leaders must find ways of aligning their wills with God's will. The individual unity in the Spirit will find unity and purpose collectively in the church. Remember the biblical teachings on the work of the Spirit:

"No one can come to me unless drawn by the Father."
"Not by might, nor by power, but by my spirit."
"You will receive power when the Holy Spirit has come upon you."

Conversion comes through the Spirit and happens at a point in time and over time through experiences with others and encounters with the Father. I often speak of many mini-conversions as a way God has worked in my Christian journey. How will God work in the church to make us into more of who God desires us to be? What are the phases/steps in the conversion of the church?

A unique challenge today and certainly in the next decade is to rethink the way we talk about, work with, and teach conversion in this unchurched culture. Not only do we need to give thought to this in our witnessing/evangelism efforts in the pagan culture, but in our church culture as well. The church has become "unchurched" in that all too often its activities, budgets, agendas, and mission are not in line with God's teachings or will for God's people. To what areas must the church be sensitive as it moves toward being a converted people?

First, consider the phases involved in converting the church. Conversion begins with a sense of brokenness and repentance, whether of the individual or the church. In an unchurched culture we are having to back up the process to helping people understand and experience their own brokenness. Our culture has become so pluralistic and diverse, in terms of belief systems and values, that we have lost not only the definition of sin, but also the definitions of lostness and brokenness. It is as if every culture is maximizing defense mechanisms to make its belief system appropriate. Somehow God's design or desire never figures into this formula. The same is true even within the church, often even among the most faithful of its leaders. We rationalize and justify our beliefs, values, and traditions without giving much consideration, if any, to God's desires or design.

We must discover ways to mirror God's reality before individuals and churches, to help reassess our definitions of success and effectiveness. Somehow we must struggle with these issues more than we struggle with personal agendas, comforts, or even the traditions of a family, congregation, or community. The church was not created *for* the community; it was created *to be* a community of faith. The church was not created for the Christian's comfort; it was created as a channel to evangelize and redeem a lost and hurting world. How can we mirror these realities? Consider the following suggestions.

- Begin each committee meeting by raising the biblical call to the Christian church.
- Ask regularly, of leaders and congregations, how we are doing in light of God's call/mission.
- Build in accountability systems for committees, classes, budgets, and programs to help insure that our comfort, needs, and agendas do not take priority.
- Be intentional about raising the biblical standards to every age group as a way of assessing, evaluating, and creating guideposts.

•Ask the congregation and community regularly to assess effectiveness and focus. Four questions might be helpful: (1) What has been the focus of our congregation the last six months to a year? (2) Has our talk matched our walk? (3) What biblical evidence is there to support and inform our direction and mission? (4) What adjustments should you/we make to be more pleasing to God's desire and design?

Another phase of conversion is commitment to follow, in order to develop the Christlike habits needed to assume leadership in pursuing Christlike behaviors, goals, attitudes, and mission. Commitment involves decision. We must decide corporately to follow Jesus with no turning back. We must decide that his mission is more important than our agendas or needs. We must decide that our mission is to be involved in his mission. These decisions will keep us stable and focused in times of instability and wandering or when strong or weak leaders are guilty of pushing personal agendas.

Developing Christlike habits for a congregation need not be difficult, but they are. Habits that follow Christ's servanthood, self-giving, compassion, denial of self, and inclusiveness are the ideal. Christ calls us to serve those inside the fold of the church, but also to leave the ninety-nine to find the lost one at any cost. He calls us to love the unlovely and impure by not judging them or insulating ourselves from them. He calls us not only to go one mile, but also to go the second mile in helping others. He calls us to forgive seventy times seventy.

How does the church live out these challenges toward servanthood in this unchurched culture with unwed mothers and fathers, AIDS victims, the abused and abusers, the ethnic communities, homosexuals, and others we tend to alienate? What about denial of ourselves for the purpose of the mission? How frequently do we deny our comforts within our air-conditioned buildings and padded pews to reach out to the hurting and destitute or alien culture? Do we forego air conditioning our building or hiring another staff person needed to care for us in order to provide resources and leadership for the poor or illiterate in our community? What about balancing our giving and service between ourselves and others within our sphere of influence and

God's plan? How often do we deny our needs to help meet the needs of another? Christ calls us to die to self in order to follow and live for him. How often are we challenged and led to die to self within the church? How responsive would you be if you were led in this direction? What is your decision or commitment? In *Death of the Church*, Mike Regele expounds upon this reality:

> A decision is imminent, but it is only a decision about how the church will die. Death is inescapable. We cannot and will not avoid it. The institutional church will either choose to die, or it will choose to die in order to live.[2]

A converted church is Spirit-directed. It is modeled and led by converted people. Through his series of disciple-making books and the Training Network, Bill Hull is committed to helping return the church to its disciple-making roots.[3] He is reintroducing the church to what it takes to create healthy disciples who, in turn, create and build healthy disciple-making churches. He declares that the model of Christ with his disciples is our guide. This model can best be summarized by the following phases:

•Come unto me.
•Come follow me.
•Come be with me.
•Come and abide in me.

These are excellent guides in understanding biblical mandates for the converted individual, and they bring clarity to how converted people fashion a converted church.

For Reflection:

1. What agendas and realities guide most of your church's meetings and events?
2. What are the advantages and disadvantages of mirroring God's realities to most church gatherings?
3. How are you and your church living out God's agenda and mission?
4. Do you agree or disagree with the quote by Mike Regele in *Death of the Church*? Why?

Nurturing the Converted

Conversion results from God calling and drawing persons toward God's self. Conversion begins with one step and leads into a lifelong journey with a host of experiences. The same is true for the church. Converted individuals nurture the church toward God's ideal. Converted individuals create converted churches. We work to help the church become what God desires and calls it to be. A system is needed to insure that the cycle functions effectively and remains healthy in light of God's call to "go and make disciples of all nations."

Typically, in the churchgoing culture of the last several decades, the church could work within a program orientation, jumping from one class or subject matter to another, sprinkled with occasional committee meetings and an occasional special event or worship service. Today, in our secularized unchurched culture, we are faced with developing an intentional system that grows persons from who they are to who God calls them to be. It becomes a pathway to take the pagan toward Christ and Christlike behaviors and habits. It moves the broken toward healing and health and the lost toward salvation and hope. Everyone comes to Christ on their own from various places, beliefs, and life experiences. These beliefs and life experiences are much more diverse and often anti-Christian in our pluralistic society. Such unique characteristics demand a more effective system that intentionally nurtures the person in conversion.

The "come and see" phase (John 1:39) modeled in Jesus' ministry serves as a needed entry point for the converted church. Because of our unchurched culture, we must give priority to creating, targeting, and nurturing this part of disciple making. It is here where people can come, with little expectations about their knowledge or practice of Christian beliefs or values. It is here where they can explore and build relationships, friendships, values, and behaviors.

Given our community environment and socioeconomic circumstances, the "come and see" phase can be manifested in several influential ways. The system of disciple making needs to be culturally sensitive and customized to the persons targeted for Christian witness or growth. For instance, persons who have no experience with or appreciation for Christian values or the institutional church as we know it are not likely to come to the church

49

or a church-focused event. Rather, they are more likely to participate in a community-wide festival that seeks to build community among newcomers to the community or to celebrate a particular holiday. There are other possible manifestations of this phase.

(1) *Small groups are often great entry points for both churchgoers and nonchurchgoers.* Identify a need that is pinching them, and sound the call to rally those with similar needs to come together for instruction, support, and fellowship to work with this need. Examples of groups might include the following:

•adults caring for aging parents
•newcomers moving into a new community
•parents of preschool or adolescent children
•single parents
•alumnae from various schools
•persons interested in various arts/crafts
•persons interested in improving their health

(2) *Corporate educational and/or worship experiences are also valid entry points for nurturing persons inside and outside the church.* Many in our culture desire anonymity and an opportunity to visit and scope out the land without being put on the spot. Therefore, the large group is often less threatening. We must work to be friendly, but not pushy or overbearing, in order to earn their respect and the right to be heard and to make friends with them. Consider the following ideas.

•*Provide musical, drama, and worship experiences* designed to bring people together to celebrate music and the Christian community, followed by a fellowship time.
•*Plan community-wide seminars* based on focused needs (for example, divorce recovery, financial planning, making life's transitions meaningful, and other life stage emphases).
•*Schedule well-known guest speakers.* They often hook persons' interests and can help them learn the location and reputation of the church and also meet some of the church folks, while they are still exploring their interest in Christian beliefs and community.

•*Host a community event* (for example, an AA group, a senior adult daycare, a community crime watch meeting, a piano or dance recital). This is a valid way of introducing persons to the church location, reputation, and membership. It also communicates to the unchurched the church's concern about issues of the community. The possibilities are limitless. Be certain to use the opportunity to build relationships in nonthreatening ways and to present a caring image via bulletin boards, bulletins, and information packets about the church.

(3) *Fellowship circles* (for example, sports teams, walking clubs, tour groups, travel clubs) are essential tools for cultivating friendships, networking, and providing entry points to a loving environment as a first step toward evangelizing those with little interest in Christ but a real interest in and need for fellowship. These groups must be intentional about reaching out to the unchurched rather than just planning for church fellowship.

Many churches would find these suggestions a major shift in their priorities for time, energy, money, and leadership. Typically they would spend hours in planning, prayer, and committee meetings designing, promoting, training for, and financing experiences for themselves. While this is a vital part of church life for many, it is not the purpose and mission of the church. The biblical mission of the church is to go into all the world, to provide "sight to the blind, to let the oppressed go free" (Luke 4:18), to feed the hungry and to visit the imprisoned (Matt 25), to praise the name of the Lord (Acts 19:17).

Such a shift of priorities represents part of the conversion I believe Christ is calling the church to. This shift calls us to:

•Refocus our committee meetings from caring for "us" to reaching "them"
•Reallocate our resources from caring for our wishes and desires to fulfilling Christ's mission among the lost, broken, and wounded of our community and world
•Reaffirm God's calling and mandate for the people of God rather than just reaffirming our history and traditions
•Redeem our time and energies for the purpose of God rather than for our self-centered agendas

•Recharge our batteries for ministry in tough times by discovering our calling, giftedness, and mission in the traditional church or in the world as a Christian leader

Most churches ignore or simply do not understand the need for this early phase of disciple making. Churches are often found saying in unison, "If they (the unchurched, uncommitted) loved Jesus more, they would come to our meetings at our prescribed times and would use our church language." This attitude alone is a significant barrier to nurturing our secularized, unchurched society into the Christian faith and community. We must understand that a different society demands a variety of approaches to ministry and church.

The ministry of Jesus certainly provides clear guidance and encouragement for this type of ministry in a secularized world to a diverse group of people and beliefs. The "come and follow me" phase of his ministry with his disciples unfolds in Mark 1:16-20. In this phase Jesus modeled for his disciples how to live the Christian life. This was an intense time of training, accountability, modeling, teaching, and learning as well as a time of discovering gifts, ministries, and the spiritual disciplines that allowed them to remain strong in their faith and witness. Jesus did not have classrooms, church buildings, record-keeping systems, computers, or printed study guides or literature. Rather he was battling against traditions and norms of his culture and seeking to introduce new Christian belief systems, role models, values, and ethics.

Most churches have focused much time and energy on this phase over the last several decades. They have designed programs, seminars, and structures that have worked effectively for most of the membership of persons with deep appreciation and respect for Christianity, the church, the Bible, religious traditions, traditional family models, and denominational loyalty. Today, these loyalties and frames of reference are so askew that even the way the church approaches this phase of Christian formation is calling for reassessment. Consider these questions and possibilities.

•What is the role of technology in our curricula design, networking, learning, and training models?

•What are the future benefits, trends, and cautions of "cyber-church" (a model of pastoring/teaching via the internet and computers)?

•How do we achieve a balance between being technologically in touch, respectful, relational, personally connected, and nurturing?

•Can nurture and training happen through the Web?

•Can training, learning, and Christian formation happen in ways and structures beyond what we currently rely on and treasure? In fact, can this formation be even more effective in other models and structures?

•What are the new forms of Christian education and spiritual life formation in this technological age?

•How can the "come and follow me" phase of spiritual formation occur in this secular age to insure more effective Christians who impact their world for the cause of Christ?

•What training and learning might occur?

(1) *Utilize media as a teaching/learning tool.* Since our culture is so influenced by the media, can we utilize this media for the purposes of teaching? We not only can, but we must learn how effectively to utilize these avenues. Many companies are already producing Christian videos and movies, while some churches and ministries are tapping into the television industry.

What if we tapped into distance learning and utilized cable television to offer a time of reflection, commentary, and teaching preceding and/or following everything from the nightly news, family movies, and prime time shows to Saturday morning cartoons? What if we helped the family take some intentional time to reflect on this media to evaluate, learn from, or react to Christian beliefs? What if a similar time of reflection was built into the Internet to help persons visiting web sites do some theological reflection on what they visit? If those who choose to do such reflection have the ability and opportunity to network together in an online seminar or a support group gathering, which would become the learning community and place of faith formation?

What if we tapped into computer-driven learning via CD ROMs or the Internet? What if topics/issues with which the world is exploring and struggling had an intentional design to help people learn to do theological reflection? What would happen if all those Christians, or searchers, who use the computer in vocation or schooling had the opportunity to do theological reflection while online and onsite? Some say that the next theological seminary will be in the workplace. The computer could make this possible if the church begins to design and affirm these structures as viable ways of Christian education.

Now I can hear many saying, the computer is not a viable option for everyone. What about that group? Precisely, we must entertain more options for educational structures and programming. However, to ignore the possibilities of technology in Christian education/formation is to put blinders on that can further feed the thoughts of many that the church is antiquated, out-of-date, and irrelevant to current issues and trends.

(2) *Utilize theological reflection in daily life events and experiences.* Grouping together persons with similar experiences and helping them process and reflect on God's work in the midst of their life is certainly a needed educational experience in our diverse culture. Providing a forum for seekers to ask probing questions, to sift through their confusions, or to help Christians find God at work in the midst of challenging situations is much needed. Groups might include:

- blended families
- unwed mothers/fathers
- victims of abuse
- victims of crime
- survivors of suicide
- parents struggling with teens
- teens struggling with parents

"How do you know which growth phase persons are in, and who makes this call?" is a frequently asked question and concern. An approach to helping each member of your congregation or group assess him/herself regarding the phases of discipleship is described in the writings of Bill Hull in *The Disciplemaking Church: Jesus Christ, the Disciplemaker.* (See "Activating the Process of Discipleship" in the appendix.)

Does this approach sound unusual for Christian formation study groups? Such is representative of our problem and a call for conversion. Our traditional study groups are formal, teacher-led, and biblical-content centered. While there is a place for this didactic approach to Bible study, ever-changing circumstances call us to provide biblical insights and values to everyday life experiences. "The Stewardship of Life" (see appendix) is illustrative of how theological reflection might occur around common life events and experiences. Take note of some of the basic questions that help persons find God at work in their life story.

This guide sheet can easily be adapted to help any age group begin to reflect on life events or experiences. Such is a significant step in Christian formation as well as in causing Christians or seekers to integrate Christian values and/or principles into their everyday life. A life that has relevancy is motivated to learn more and provides an opportunity to network with others of similar concerns, challenges, and/or commitments. These are the Sunday School classes, discipleship groups, and mission groups of the future.

For Reflection:

1. How are you emotionally responding to these possibilities?
2. What possibilities can you envision?
3. What barriers need to be addressed?

Producing Healthy Disciples

The biblical picture of the church is filled with challenge, courage, risk taking, relationships, and witness. The essence of the New Testament church is to make disciples, or followers of Christ. Over the centuries, however, through various sociopolitical challenges and changes, our culture has become more diverse and pluralistic. Families have taken on different shapes. Dysfunction has become a household word. Thus it is becoming more and more difficult for the church, as we know it, to produce healthy disciples. Most current disciples are rather unhealthy. Either we as the church are not producing, or when we do, we produce persons who have poor understandings of the Christian faith and the church tradition and who have little or no influence on their world for Christ. Our membership is declining, our effectiveness is almost nil, and the membership is saying that church is boring, dull, and irrelevant. I would say we have a problem!

Our programmatic, church-centered, time-oriented approach to Christian education frequently produces followers whose faith and loyalty are more often bound to religious places and times than to the challenges of a pagan society. The Christianity of the New Testament was not bound by institutions or time frames, but by one's personal walk with Christ. It was the abiding relationship with Christ that produced "much fruit."

The old church is passing away; the new church is being created. Someone has said that the church is dying—and God is killing it in order to create something new. There are grains of truth in this saying. Unless the church we have known and loved (which is too often limited to traditional time frames, orders of worship, and institutional programs) passes away, the mission of the church may be lost. Today, we are working with technology, cyberspace, intercontinental travel, cellular phones, fax machines, and instantaneous television coverage anywhere in the world. How can the Christian message be taught and lived out in such a culture? When distance learning is the current trend in adult higher education, what is the church's response? Are we going to continue to ask our adults to come to meetings, scheduled only one time a week, at one site, when there are many other avenues available for training and networking persons?

Recently I visited and worshiped with the First Church of Cyberspace. Via the Internet, I listened in on a committee of persons scattered across the globe who were planning a drama for corporate worship in Chicago the following Sunday. I dialogued with a group of managers, via conference call, about how business managers can be the "presence of Christ" in their workplace and bear fruit for the kingdom in and through their work. These are issues and avenues we cannot ignore nor seek to incorporate into the way we do church. What does all this have to do with making healthy disciples?

Healthy disciples are fruit-bearing disciples, effective in translating scriptural truth into their daily lives. If life today is so tied to technology, we cannot ignore it or pretend it does not exist. If the public sector, business sector, and educational systems are utilizing and benefiting from distance learning and computer-driven presentations, do we really believe that parents, children, and youth are going to come to a church where little or no technology is utilized in worship and education? We are certainly privileged to be pioneers for the new church.

In the August 1996 edition of *The Atlantic Monthly*, a secular magazine, the lead article was entitled, "Welcome to the Next Church." Let me share some quotes to wet your appetite and give clarity to elements of a converted church that is serious about producing healthy disciples.

> No spires. No crosses. No robes. No clerical collars. No hard pews. No kneelers. No biblical gobbledygook. No prayerly rote. No fire, no brimstone. No pipe organs. No dreary eighteenth-century hymns. No forced solemnity. No Sunday finery. No collection plates.[4]

> Social institutions that once held civic life together—schools, families, governments, companies, neighborhoods, and even old-style churches—are not what they used to be. The new congregations are reorganizing religious life to fill that void.[5]

> We give them what they want, "and we give them what they didn't know they wanted—a life change."

> What is our business? Turning irreligious or unchurched people into fully devoted followers of Christ.[6]

> Next church services are multimedia affairs.[7]

These quotes and many others represent the tenor of this article and the movement of redefinition of church that is occurring in our society. The megachurches summarized are serious about Christianity, making disciples, penetrating the unchurched culture for Christ, and taking their Christian faith into the world. They have discovered that disciple making requires the church to do several things.

- Be attractive to nonbelievers. Use language, structures, and curricula that are not threatening but attractive.
- Be relevant and meaningful to believers and nonbelievers alike.
- Offer multiple opportunities that are appropriate to the phase of spiritual formation persons are currently experiencing.
- Show a willingness to meet people where they are rather than where we would prefer them to be (for example, in terms of their relationships, morals, ethics, behaviors, status).
- Provide opportunities for all persons to feel significant and meaningful through their involvement in ministry and spiritual life reflection.
- Create a church that speaks, teaches, and ministers in ways that are meaningful to the targeted people group(s) rather than a church that preserves religious traditions or personal dreams.

Making disciples in the modern age requires the church to take seriously each person's culture, background, educational level, interest in spirituality, and phase of Christian growth. The church can no longer treat everyone the same or offer the same resource materials or the same learning or discipling structure. People have varying needs, styles of learning, and time availabilities. Disciplemaking is a must, a biblical mandate, a necessity for pleasing God and fulfilling God's plan. The way disciples are made should be culture-sensitive and customized to the learner. Remember the earlier phases of disciple making: "come and see"; "come and follow me." Each is vital to the process, yet each has very unique features and characteristics to plan for and consider.

The "abide in me" phase, as explained by Hull, describes those who have matured in their faith, exercised leadership, and proven the ability to "go it alone" in ministering to others. This phase is the fruit-bearing time, the lifelong journey of ministry that for the original disciples was without the physical presence of Christ or other mentors. What does the church do to network, affirm, mature, and nurture those abiding in Christ?

Too often the remnant is ignored by the clergy and the church, thus becoming weakened and fruitless. If the church is to produce healthy disciples, it must not ignore those who are hungry, searching for God's will and presence, and asking the right questions. The new church must have a relevant plan to address the four phases of Christian formation. While the traditional Sunday School class format may still have a place, the church must develop its Christian education model to go far beyond the Sunday morning classroom. Other models of Christian education must include several of the following opportunities for small groups of persons in various phases of formation.

- Computer-driven educational programs for individual group or family use
- Internet web sites for various vocational groupings who are seeking to flesh out their faith in the workplace; web pages designed as a Christian education forum
- Audio library consisting of books, seminars, and conferences on tape with learning sheets, accountability, and relationships
- Video library that is topical and focused
- Distance learning consisting of forums, computer seminars, and access to networking with others who have similar concerns or interest
- Community groupings that are comfortable with a low threat level as entry points to discipling relationships

For Reflection:

1. What are the characteristics of healthy disciples?
2. What are the characteristics of the disciples being created by your church currently? What are the future plans?
3. What do you feel about this chapter's content?
4. What suggestions do you have concerning this topic?
5. What is your church, and your life, reproducing? What kind of Christians are you producing by your activities, worship, discipling, and so on?

Conclusion

While visiting a coffee shop, which was the place for meetings in the city, I found myself in "Internet heaven" with warm, friendly people who were connecting not only with the Net, but with each other around common interests, passions, and concerns. I sat by myself, ordered my latte, and almost immediately my waiter introduced himself and asked if I had any interest in the Net as well as how he might be able to help. He wanted to help me learn to tap into the information I desired and then to network with others via cyberspace and the coffee house patrons who shared similar interests. Before I left, I had made friends, felt encouraged, learned new skills, struggled with my learning curve, and found hope in the help of others and the information highway. While doing this I enjoyed several inspiring and ministry-focused conversations with strangers who became friends. One was struggling with loneliness in the big city, and another shared my passion for ministry in the workplace.

A friend of mine came into town. I had spent several hours via the phone talking him through personal crises of faith and belief. Due to a storm, he became stranded at the airport. God allowed us to meet for a casual meal, followed by a four-hour conversation and walk in which he found insights into himself, his family of origin, and God's desire for his life. The tears flowed, and the hugs brought comfort, security, and affirmation. When we departed that evening, he said to me, "Thanks Eddie. I feel I have worshiped and encountered God's presence tonight." I got into my car and said, "Yes! We did church!"

The converted church recognizes that conversion demands introspection, self-evaluation, and acknowledgment of sin and shortcomings followed by a refocusing of priorities and energies. Conversion takes time, effort, and the guiding presence of the Spirit of God drawing us toward God and the divine plan and will for God's people.

For Reflection:

1. What is the Spirit saying to you?
2. What is your respose to these new insights and/or convictions?
3. Who do you need to share these insights and convictions with?

Notes

[1]Walter Brueggeman, Lecture at Landue Chapel, Missouri, summarized in *Kirkwood Kindler*, 29 October 1996.

[2]Mike Regele, *Death of the Church* (Grand Rapids: Zondervan, 1995)

[3]For additional information, contact Bill Hull, T-NET International (1-800-995-5362). This organization, more than any I know, offers a process approach that helps clergy and lay leaders learn skills for customizing church to be effective in our secular culture.

[4]Charles Truehart, "Welcome to the Next Church," *The Atlantic Monthly*, 1 August 1996, 37.

[5]Ibid., 38.

[6]Ibid., 40.

[7]Ibid., 42.

Making the Church of Tomorrow Work

From Program Development to Faith Formation

The apostle Paul and the disciple Peter had earth-shaking, life-changing insights that led to their repentance and conversion. Likewise, the institutional church is challenged to new insights and possibly its own personal and corporate repentance and/or conversion to enable the will and plan of God to become more effective in this pagan culture.

From the late 1950s to the mid 1970s, our culture responded well to a program-based model for Christian education and church life. Our culture responded effectively to printed and mass-produced curricula, organizational development, diversified task assignments, and a centralized model of church. Then technology, diversification, and pluralism of values and cultures rapidly assaulted our churched culture with its safe, predictable programs.

Today the established programs are found wanting and irrelevant for many, including those who have been active in the church for years. There is a real hunger for spirituality and faith formation in our midst, accompanied by a fading interest in institutionalized, program-based, centralized approaches to church and Christianity. The baby boomers who returned to church by the droves are now leaving and calling the church ineffective and irrelevant.[1] The senior adult population continues to be loyal to what has nurtured and loved them, but even their morals, faith formation, and biblical knowledge are weak in many respects. People are networking to explore spiritual thirsts, but the groups do not seem to have ties to the traditional approaches of church.

What are these and many other trends telling us about how to share the Good News effectively in this pagan yet spiritually thirsty culture? These issues fuel and inform the call for the conversion of the church. Here are some practical tips for refashioning the church for the 21st century.

(1) *Enlist, activate, and equip faith formation directors rather than program directors.* These will serve as spiritual guides, directors, and catalysts for integrating biblical truths into daily life experiences. We must enlist leaders who have a passion to help persons of all ages integrate their faith life with their daily life. Leaders must be willing to walk with the hurting, wounded, and searching of our world as we seek to discover and follow God in our midst. Faith formation directors should be:

- Trusted disciples who exhibit maturity of faith in their own lives
- Disciples who exhibit servanthood behavior and attitude rather than power or spiritual elitism
- Willing to spend quality time in mentoring, apprenticing, or accountability relationships with those searching or in need
- Willing to work to help the searchers find appropriate questions that help integrate faith and life rather than providing answers
- Skilled at facilitating a learning process for the searcher rather than trying to teach the student truths he/she has for them
- Intentional about helping the searcher assess spiritual issues in their lives and relationships while developing skills to discover nurture for themselves through prayer, study, reflection, and confession
- Discerning of God's leading and timing within the spiritual relationship

The culture is calling forth spiritual companions for the life journey.[2] Certainly the Christian faith knows this model. Think of Abraham, the father of our faith whom God called to go to a place he knew not. God called him to walk by faith and found others who could walk with him toward obedience and faithfulness. God called him and calls us to be a blessing.

(2) *Teach stewardship of life rather than stewardship of resources.* Many of those in our pagan culture, as well as a few in our churched culture, accuse the church of "just being after their money." This attitude springs from our teaching of the tithe and the stewardship of our resources. Scripture calls us to teach stewardship of all of life rather than just our resources. In Romans 12, Paul calls us to present our bodies a living sacrifice. In Corinthians, he calls us to "do all that we do for the glory of God." Jesus calls us to "give ourselves" and not turn back. The unchurched culture is challenging the church to convert its thinking and expectations to this biblical truth.

When the church returns to teaching and modeling the stewardship of life rather than just resources, I suspect we will see a growth in not only budgets, but also in commitment as disciples. By reducing stewardship to the giving of money, the church has minimized the virtues and callings of the Christian faith, thus sabotaging their vital impact. The church must help people learn to tell their story, to discover God in their lives, to determine how to be more obedient to God in their daily walk and how to live their lives as a gift to God and as Christ's visible presence in the world. See "The Stewardship of Life" in the appendix for an example of how some of the goals might be examined as the church struggles to convert from teaching about stewardship of resources to teaching the stewardship of life.

(3) *Be Spirit-led rather than structure-led.* The diversification, pluralism, and skepticism of our day challenge us to listen carefully to the leadership of the Holy Spirit in order to effectively contextualize, but not change, the message of the Good News. While contextualization is vital in our day, it is equally necessary to insure that the message of the Good News is not altered. Often in the past the church has relied too heavily on secure, predictable program structures, language, and curricula to guide growth and ministry. The church must move beyond these certainties to rediscover stability, focus, and clarity from the Spirit's leadership rather than from the structures of the institutional church alone.

Church leaders must be encouraged to listen more to the voice of the Lord than to the dictates of boards. Leaders must be found in their prayer closets more frequently than in their planning councils. They must be found tuning their ears to spiritual things rather than to structural traditions.

For Reflection:

1. How would you summarize this section?
2. What are your feelings about these issues as they relate to your personal life and/or church?
3. Why are these issues important for refashioning the church for the 21st century?

From Church Focus to World Focus

"God so loved the world that he gave his only Son" (John 3:16). God left us not to be of the world but to be in the world as representatives (John 15:18-25). We are God's disciples to be salt, light, and leaven in the world (Matt 5:14f). Somewhere in our ecclesiastical history we have shifted away from the biblical mandate and now act as though God cares more for the church than for the world. Even though the church is the bride of Christ, God sent His son to die for the world.

Our current culture seems to be calling us to shift from our concern for preserving the institutional church as we know it to penetrating the world with the message of Christ. This is the call of Christ as well as the challenge for the Christian church of the 21st century. This conversion includes a shift from teaching and training to learning and equipping, from a curricula-driven to a mission-driven church, from productivity to effectiveness. Suggestions for accomplishing these changes follow.

(1) *Focus on learning and equipping rather than on teaching and training.* My seminary training and my church experience as a layperson have focused on helping me learn to teach and train persons to operate the church programs (for example, be a good Sunday School teacher, committee member, or missions leader). Today we are told that we must focus moreso on learning and equipping. This shift is succinctly described in the following chart.[3]

Training	Learning
Goal is training	Goal is to produce learning
Teacher-focused	Learner-focused
Teacher's role is expert	Teacher's role is coach, facilitator
Learner's role is passive	Learner's role is active
Individual	Team/community/collaborative
Program-driven	Process-driven
Standardized	Customized
Linear, sequential	Experiential, relationship-based
Periodic, as needed	Continuous, lifelong
Long-term semester	Short-term, retreats, seminars
Classroom-located	Learning environment-located
Memorize information	Critical thinking, problem solving
Feedback is a test for retention	Feedback is a test for application

This conversion toward a focus on learning and equipping rather than on teaching and training will be difficult at best for most churches and church leaders. Our definition of church is so standardized and centralized that we have national curriculum publishing houses to service our churches, and until recently all studied the same text and lesson at the same time. We even have annual church profiles that count the number of persons who attend our programs in our buildings as a primary determinant of our success. The shift toward counting other things has begun and will continue to offer challenges in the decades to come.

Traditionally the church has enlisted teachers for Bible study classes that meet in the church at a set time for the purpose of learning facts for retention. The leadership has trained teachers how to organize for outreach and inreach, but they continue to have few unchurched persons in their classes. Emerging Bible study trends are issue-oriented, life-focused, and facilitated by one who desires to see these biblical truths integrated into the life of the group members. Such study occurs at a convenient time but not necessarily at the church. Numbers in attendance do not count; the focus is on how these students make a difference in the world for the cause of Christ. Do you see the difference?

Evaluate your class or group in light of the suggested shift from teaching to learning. Return to the chart and place a check beside each characteristic that best represents your class and/or group. Then circle those characteristics that best represent your leadership objectives and/or style.

(2) *Cultivate a mission-driven church rather than a curricula-driven church.* Because we have been a denominationally loyal group of persons, we have typically ordered printed literature from our national agencies and boards and have tried to be cooperative churches—all working "off the same page." Now due to increased diversity, cultural context, and need for customization, the curricula is being more contextualized than ever before. Local leaders are designing curricula to accomplish the local church's mission, rather than just the mission of the denomination. In fact, because our culture is becoming less and less denominationally loyal, the definition and scope of curriculum is changing. We are having to learn to design a mission-driven curriculum rather

than a curricula-driven curriculum. Evaluate your church's curriculum in light of the following criteria:

•Is the curriculum effective in your church? Is the church producing healthy, knowledgeable disciples because of what it is doing in church programming?
•What is the mission of your church? Do the activities in the various meetings and organizations help accomplish this mission? Why or why not?
•How do you feel about making this shift? What benefits do you see? What barriers do you see?

(3) *Define success as effectiveness rather than as activity and productivity.* Churches evaluate success based on how many participate in the programs, the number of buildings, the size of the budget, and the number of paid staff. The larger the numbers, the more successful. As the church moves into the 21st century and works within a secular culture, however, it must define success in a different manner. Church leaders must look at how effective we are in accomplishing the biblical mission. How effective are we at penetrating the world for the cause of Christ? Consider the following evaluation standards:

•How many persons involved in Bible study took the truths into their workplace, community, and/or family life and made a difference?
•How many believers are intentional about building witnessing relationships with nonbelievers?
•How much money from the church budget has been spent on building the institutional church versus the amount of money spent on ministering to and reaching the unchurched in the community?
•How many individuals and/or families have become involved in mission projects outside the church walls?
•How many persons seeking to break unhealthy life patterns (for example, addictions, dysfunctional relationships) are in recovery?
•How many newcomers (those who have attended less than one year) are involved in the leadership circles of the congregation?

•How many established members have become friends and/or mentors to newcomers and/or new converts in the past year?

•How many networks of relationships have been created for the unchurched or the searching to help them become assimilated into the life of the congregation?

•How many newlywed couples have been counseled and paired with another couple in a marriage mentoring relationship?

•How many new persons have entered the leadership circle over the past year?

•How many unchurched persons are being intentionally touched by the life of the class/group/church?

•How many hours have been spent in prayer, reflection, and seeking God's will for the life of the congregation?

•How many have moved into the leadership circle from the passive pew sitters, new church members, and others?

These are only representative questions we as the church need to ask as we seek to be effective in accomplishing the Great Commission. We must begin counting, recording, and celebrating those things we believe are important for accomplishing our mission. We must begin to focus on the life of our organization and let go of events, activities, and resources that are distracting us from accomplishing our mandates as the people of God.

Our years of trying to be more active and productive (offering more programs, bigger buildings, and bigger budgets) have drained our energies and resources and have diversified our loyalties from the Great Commission to building a church. We must recommit ourselves to fulfilling the Great Commission and to concerning ourselves with effectiveness instead of activity and productivity.

For Reflection:

1. What are your feelings about this section?

2. What realizations and convictions have you arrived at by reading this material?

3. What is the Spirit leading you to do with these realizations and convictions?

From Success to Effectiveness

The standards for evaluation must be converted by church leaders and congregational members alike. In past years leaders were affirmed, rewarded, and even advanced based on the "bigger is better" syndrome. More people in Sunday School, worship, or the choir was most often seen as successful. In the world of tomorrow, success will be based not on just how many are present, but on the effectiveness of what transpires during the gathering. The standards for tomorrow will center around issues such as the following:

- How did the Bible study content impact the daily lives of the participants in their decision making, business negotiations, and family relationships? Are the participants now less likely to be angered, less likely to be passive in the face of secularism, and more nurturing of family members?
- What Christian values were enhanced and acted upon due to participation in worship?
- How many unchurched are being touched by the programming of the church?

Since the standards for success are shifting to effectiveness and away from business as usual, numbers of laypersons are being called to accountability and responsibility for the life and effectiveness of the church. No longer can the success of the church be relegated to the church staff alone. Effectiveness will be determined when the entire congregation becomes involved in, active in, and committed to fleshing out their Christian faith in every area of their lives. No longer should laypersons elect to dismiss their ministerial staff because of the poor numbers in attendance or the declining budget. Rather, members of the congregation will have to look deeper at their effectiveness in nurturing persons in the faith, thus impacting the community for Christ through their admonitions, presence, and involvement in community and church activities. Effectiveness of the congregation fulfilling its mission might be assessed by the following standards for laypersons and clergy alike:

- How many community organizations/clubs are members actively and intentionally involved in to be the light, salt, and leaven in that group?
- How many unchurched, hurting people are being cultivated in your workplace as part of your commitment to Christ and your care for the hurting in the world?
- How many persons are intentionally working out of their call and giftedness both inside and outside the institutional church?
- How many persons are maturing in their faith in ways that their attitudes toward the poor, the diseased, the divorced, and others are more in line with that modeled by Christ?
- How many events/activities are being conducted by families, groups, and the congregation that are intentionally designed to reach out to those not already in the group(s)?

These new standards call us to move from concentrating on present members to going into the world. Heretofore the church and its leaders have focused most of their time and energy pacifying those in the pew rather than penetrating the world for the cause of Christ. As a result, people in the pew have been happy, cared for, supportive, and affirming. When leaders have not spent adequate time and attention pampering the pew people, however, these persons have become restless and often angry and hurt. Ministry such as nurturing, supporting, visiting, and recognizing the needs and desires of those in the pew ultimately creates a very introverted congregation that loses its vision and often the ability to reach out and thus fulfill the Great Commission.

Unless the standard changes from taking care of ourselves to reaching the world, the church will not be seen as effective by those outside the church—those who long to see the church reach out to them, care for them, help heal their hurts, and share the Good News with them. In an unchurched culture it is imperative that the church not spend all of its time, energy, and commitment on caring for the flock inside the church. The church must give the flock encouragement, permission, and support to "leave the ninety-nine and go find the one." In fact, I'd like to see some of our churches put their offices inside a public building or mall so that the church would be more accessible to the world than to the people who come to the church. Such a drastic step would visually represent a shift from pampering the pew to a desire and commitment to penetrate the world for Christ.

The 21st century is calling us to "be" church more than to "do" church. Most church people are unclear what we mean by this concept, however. They immediately say that they try to be good people. It is not enough to be good people. We must learn how to be God's people in an unchurched, pagan culture. How might this look? Consider the following possibilities:

•Create a network for the artistic community and involve them in some way in the life of the community and/or congregation. Celebrate their gifts and talents, and help them understand that these gifts are God-given.
•Create a group for empty nesters who are struggling with redefining their identities and strengthening their marriage after the children have gone.
•Involve and support Christians on school boards and in community groups, bowling leagues, and other organizations as representatives of Christ and his values.
•Create caregiving task forces to assist during public tragedies (for example, natural disasters and families of crime victims) and to build relationships with the medical, legal, media, and educational leaders.
•Create a job bank for the unemployed of the community. Organize the body of Christ to help others design resumes and refine interview and job skills. Build a network among Christian businesspeople who will match jobs with those in need.
•Minister through presence to those who are lonely, hurting, and afraid (for example, those who are ill and have no family, those who are afraid of being homeless and have no one to talk to or care for them).

Are you beginning to catch on to the shift from doing to being? These illustrations certainly would activate the body of Christ. They do not suggest that we be self-serving in our doing, but that we attempt to be among the hurting, the poor, the needy, and the lost. We must put ourselves among the unchurched. They will not come to us until we learn to go to them in ways that communicate the care, compassion, and concern of Christ.

For Reflection:

1. How do you feel about this shifting of the success model?
2. Answer each of the following questions for yourself and for the church and/or class of which you are a member:

    (a) Where did you find Christ at work in the world?
    (b) What was he doing?
    (c) How did you or could you have partnered with Christ?
    (d) How did you feel in these situations?
    (e) What did you feel a need for at that time?
    (f) What do you need from the body of Christ?
    (g) What biblical story gives you guidance and help?

From Gathered Church to Scattered Church

Biblical images refer to both the gathered church and the scattered church— "the bride of Christ," "the people of God," "the family of God," "a royal priesthood," "flock," "the body of Christ," "co-laborers together with God," "people on mission," "ministers of reconciliation," "priests." The missionary journeys of Paul indicate that the message of the gospel was not contained in a gathered place of obedient followers, but all along his journey, with people he encountered from various life circumstances. The first churches were not major institutions consuming time and resources, but rather a group of believers seeking God's will, who shared everything in common, broke bread together, and studied the apostles' doctrines (Acts 2). Frank Stagg, a respected New Testament scholar, declares, "The *ekklesia* of God refers to God's own people. Ownership, not local assembly, is the emphasis. Whose people, not where or whether assembled, is the New Testament idea."[4]

The shifts in our society are calling us to balance the way we do church. The balance needed is between the gathered church model and the scattered church model. The gathered church meets on Sundays for worship, praise, and equipping. The scattered church is the body of believers who are intentional about living out their faith in Christ throughout the week as they are "scattered into the world." The gathered church must scatter so as to penetrate the world for Christ Monday through Saturday in work, community clubs, leisure activities, and family units. After all, the scattered church is where 90 percent of the church's work is accomplished. It is where the hurting are helped, the aimless are counseled, the bereaved are comforted, the imprisoned are visited, the naked are clothed, the lost are witnessed to, and the hungry are fed.

The challenge for Christians of the next century is to learn how to bear fruit for the kingdom of God in and through daily work and relationships. The church must see itself as a "mission outpost" from which the gathered church scatters. If churches continue to see themselves as just places where God's people meet, rather than as equipping stations from which God's people work, they are destined to a continuing decline in membership and positive image in the community. Because churchgoers have been "gathered" so long, we are not only being ignored by the world, we are having little or no impact on the world for Christ. The broken, hurting, and sinful world is crying out for the church to develop an intentional ministry as the scattered church that will make a difference in the world. We must move from behind our stained glass windows into the struggles and heartaches of the people in the communities.

When we learn how to be an effective scattered church, we will discover that the unchurched will pay attention and see the difference of Christ working in us. Someone has said, "In days gone by, people would come to church for fellowship and relationships. Today people must have relationships before they come to church." This statement summarizes the value and significance of the ministry of the scattered church. If the scattered church is so significant, why has it been so overlooked in most denominations, conventions, and local congregations?

Traditionally, very little has been specifically addressed to equipping the scattered church for effective ministry for Christ in the world. There are several reasons for this trend. Most Christians have the conviction that the nature of the church is to "gather together," to maintain ecclesiastical programs, and to serve those in the congregation. Because this belief is so rampant, Christians spend most of their time looking inward and taking care of their own. Such an inward focus ignores the scattered church.

Most Christians' convictions about the nature of the church are not grounded in scripture, but in tradition of friends, forebears, and/or family. Such a foundation frequently leads church leaders and well-meaning Christians to ignore the scattered church and glorify the traditional church. It is easier to maintain ecclesiastical machinery (for example, church programs, committees, and social agendas) than to be a people on mission in the world. Building a church program certainly has its place in the nature of the people of God, but it is not the mission of the people of God. Building a church to make a difference in the world for Christ is the mission of God's people.

Our standards of success as a church are guided by the wrong concepts of what it means to be the people of God. Most churches, church staff, and church leaders are evaluated on how many people come to the church programs, rather than how many go from the church and make a difference in the world. The key issue of success for the church is not just how many people come to the church, but rather how many actually are equipped to be the church in their daily lives.

The inward focus of many of our churches has created much of the apathy we see in our churches. The people of God want to be challenged and equipped to make a difference in the world. After years of inward focus of the church leadership, however, the committed Christians give up their dream of making a difference and fall into building and maintaining the ecclesiastical machinery.

Ignoring the needs, reality, and value of the scattered church has caused Christians not only to be introverted in their focus, but to be perceived by the world as isolationist, unconcerned, and irrelevant. If the Christian community is going to fulfill Christ's mandate to permeate the world, we must begin to understand that the scattered church is as important as the gathered church. We must therefore struggle with how to equip, support, and resource the scattered church to insure a balanced and effective ministry of the Christian church in the world.

How can we equip the scattered church? What kind of curricula does a scattered church require? What kind of leadership style is needed by the clergy to facilitate the ministry of the scattered church? How do we insure that the gathered church is relevant for the scattered church? How do we connect the ministries of the scattered church to the purpose and function of the gathered church? Such will be questions Christian leaders will grapple with for the next decades.

As we begin to identify the issues involved in designing an effective curricula for the scattered and gathered church, we must agree on several givens:

(1) The Scriptures and the movement of the Holy Spirit must be the guiding light for the design and development of this curricula.

(2) The needs of the people inside and outside the church must be clearly understood so that we might seek to answer questions being asked today, rather than work to answer questions no one is asking.

(3) We must work to insure a balance in the curricula design so that our "doing" must come out of our "being." That is to say, we must guide the believers to build the braces of faith within that which will insure energy to go the full journey in ministry as we be and do church. Often we have been guilty of only becoming a people of servant acts as we go forth to do church, rather than becoming a servant people as we go forth to be the church. Equipping the scattered church will require:

•A clearer understanding of and intentional alignment to the biblical mandate for all the people of God
•A curricula built upon the questions the Christian world and the non-Christian world are asking rather than the traditions of a church
•A support network for the scattered church that will offer emotional, physical, and spiritual support as the scattered church involves itself in ministry in the world
•An avenue of reporting and sounding the call for help in the gathered church (the scattered church needs to share needs and celebrations with the gathered Christian community)
•A clergy trained and committed to preaching to, walking with, and unleashing the scattered church as it seeks to adjust the agendas of the gathered church to acknowledge and support the scattered church
•Relational curricula focused on finding "our story" in the biblical story and experiencing a faith that makes a difference in the world
•Giving permission and encouragement to move our churches from a program-based design to a ministry-based design
•Modeling discipleship by reproducing disciples and teaching others the essentials of the faith
•Finding similarities and support in the mission and ministry of the scattered and gathered church
•Maintaining a healthy understanding between the scattered and gathered church

For too long, Christians have felt that our mission as God's people was to be faithful to "come to the church." However, God's mandate for all Christians is to go into all the world and preach, teach, and baptize. Yes, Christ is concerned that we attend church, but he and his mission are dependent on us going into the world. The mission of Christ—to redeem the world—hangs on whether believers find their ministry and mission as the scattered church. If we continue to only celebrate and resource the gathered church, we are likely to become more introverted, exclusive, and out of touch with the changing world and the cause of Christ, thus causing the future of the church to be at great risk. Therefore, the heartbeat of the church's mission is bound up in the mission of the scattered church.

For Reflection:

1. Summarize the ideas concerning the gathered and scattered church.
2. What insights and values do these concepts have for the future church?
3. Who illustrates these truths for you?

Conclusion

Doing church in the year 2000 is certain to be filled with great challenges and struggles. Not only are we faced with a broken world, filled with more heartache and temptation than ever before, but we are also faced with what appears to be a broken church, a church that has become self-centered and irrelevant. We must return to "our first love" and find creative, relevant ways to tell the Good News so that it might be heard and received.

The church of Jesus Christ has the message of hope for which the world awaits. We must continue to gather together for worship, praise, and equipping. But we also must commit ourselves to unleashing the church, at whatever cost, so that the world might know Christ and the power of his love as the church moves through the grocery stores, department stores, hospitals, business offices, and soup kitchens on a daily basis. We must move from program development to faith formation, from a church focus to a world focus, from an emphasis on success to an emphasis on effectiveness, always functioning as the scattered church.

Certainly, "the fields are white unto harvest." The problem is not with the fields, but with the reapers (the church). We have been conditioned to believe that we must bring the broken to the church to be comforted. Now we are being forced to learn how to reap the harvest in the fields (Luke 10:2f; Matt 10:16f). Go forth then and make a difference in the world for Jesus Christ!

For Reflection:

1. What is the Spirit saying to you?
2. How are you responding to these holy nudgings?
3. What are your next steps?

Notes

[1]Doug Mureen, "Boomers Leaving the Church," *Western Recorder*, 17 September 1996, 8.

[2]Linda Vogel, *Teaching and Learning in Communities of Faith* (San Francisco: Jossey-Bass, 1991).

[3]Carol Childress, "Shifting from Training to Learning," NetFax, Leadership Network, Tyler TX.

[4]Frank Stagg, *New Testament Theology* (Nashville: Broadman Press, 1962) 181.

Converting the Church for the 21st Century

The Need for New Wineskins

The world is changing more rapidly than ever. Yet, most churches seem to be stuck in time, clinging to tradition and structures at the expense of fulfilling the biblical mission. Dietrich Bonhoeffer declared,

> The church is the church only when it exists for others. To make a start, it should give away all its property to those in need. The clergy must live solely on the freewill offerings of their congregations, or possibly engage in some secular calling. The church must share in the secular problems of ordinary human life, not dominating, but helping and serving. It must tell men of every calling what it means to live in Christ, to exist for others.[1]

Based on this definition of the church, we must be honest and say that when churchgoers and nonchurchgoers look at the church of today, they see a major discrepancy between what should be and what is. If the church exists for others, then what are the needs of others? If the church is not fulfilling its mission, what adjustments need to be made to insure that the church has a significant role in the 21st century?

The words of Jesus are taking on new significance during these days of change in society and the church. He said, "No one puts new wine into old wineskins, for the new wine bursts the old skins, ruining the skins and spilling the wine. New wine must be put into new wineskins" Luke 5:37-38 (Living Bible). What did Jesus mean, and how does his instruction inform the church of today and tomorrow?

The parable of the wineskins teaches us that God is a God of newness. The Old Testament frequently speaks of new things. We read of a new song, a new heart, a new spirit, a new name, a new covenant, a new creation, and so on (Ps 40:3; Isa 42:9, 43:19; Ezek 11:19). The New Testament supports this view as it reveals God will make all things new (Rev 21:5) and that the gospel is the "new and living way" (Heb 10:20).

Every age knows the temptation to forget that the gospel is ever new. We try to contain the new wine of the gospel in old wineskins—outmoded traditions, obsolete philosophies, creaking institutions, and old habits. But with time, the old wineskins begin to bind the gospel. Then they must burst, and the power of the gospel will pour forth once more. New wineskins become necessary. Wineskins are not eternal. As time passes, they must be replaced, not because the gospel changes, but because the gospel itself demands and produces change. New wine must be put into new wineskins.[2]

Certainly, Jesus who gave us the biblical mission of the church allowed for and encouraged change of the wineskins in order to preserve the wine (the message and mission). Why then has the church been so reluctant to change?

Much of the church's reluctance to change issues from the fact that the church is made up of human beings who really do not like change. All of us like to live in our comfort zones. In other words, we have met the enemy, and it is us! The church is reluctant to change because of its focus on the institution and those who attend.

(I) *We have been more concerned about building an institution than about building the church.* The Protestant Reformation challenged and changed our understanding of salvation (soteriology), but it hardly touched our doctrine of church (ecclesiology).[3] Because our ecclesiology was basically untouched by the Reformation, we are still trying to define church by "building temples" or "erecting tabernacles." The erecting of tabernacles in the Old Testament was a symbol of God's presence (Exod 25:8). The idea was that God's habitation was with the people (God became mobile). God could not actually dwell in the hearts of the people, however, due to their sin and rebelliousness.[4] Therefore, the temple was built. It was permanent and stationary (1 Kgs 6:12-13). The temple was permitted by God to be built by David, but the temple was not God's idea.

Today's Christians have picked up on the tabernacle and/or temple understanding of church without understanding fully the New Testament concept of church. According to Acts 7:44-48, "The Most High does not dwell in houses made with hands." Theologically, the church does not need temples. Church buildings are not essential to the true nature of the church.[5] This reason, probably more than any other, accounts for why the church is so reluctant to change. We still believe that we please God by building our buildings.

(2) *The church has been more focused on those inside the walls than those outside the walls.* Members of the Christian community believe that the church was created for them, when in reality the church is the only organization in society created for those outside it. When we turned inward and started caring only for each other, we lost sight of the poor and hurting of society (most of whom are not involved in an institutional church). Instead of keeping abreast of needs in our society, we spent our time, money, and energy taking care of us! After doing this for so long, we found that we liked being taken care of by those we know and trust. We became insulated or isolated from those to whom Christ calls the church to minister.

Our problem is internal in that the church is its own worst enemy. We have become too comfortable, too self-serving, and too ignorant of the society in which we are called to minister. John Havlik and John Westerhoff provide us with a challenge as we seek to align ourselves to the biblical mandate and reshape the church for the 21st century. Havlick explains,

> The church is never a place, but always a people; never a fold, but always a flock; never a sacred building, but always a believing assembly. The church is you who pray, not where you pray. A structure of brick or marble can no more be a church than your clothes of serge or satin can be you. There is in this world nothing sacred but man, no sanctuary of man but the soul.[6]

Westerhoff elaborates,

> To be God's child is to be creative. To be creative is to acknowledge and work with conflict and tension. To live faithfully on journey is to live with unsettledness and change. If God's people are to live with this continual process of conversion, this ongoing struggle of bringing order out of chaos, then the church's task becomes to confront and to cause dis-ease, rather than to permit its members to escape through a superficial peace of mind.[7]

When evaluating the present-day church in light of these two observations, it seems that we have succeeded at creating good church members but poor Christians.

The problem is real. The challenge is an opportunity to make a difference. How then do we go about reshaping the church for the future? We must understand future trends in society that will impact the church, recommit ourselves to being the church rather than just building the church, and design a plan to move the church from where we are to where God desires us to go.

For Reflection:

1. "New wineskins" is a biblical idea. What new wineskins have you encountered in your church over the past year?
2. Why do you believe churches focus most of their time, energy, and money inside the walls, when the Great Commission is clear that the church is to reach beyond the walls?

The Challenge of Future Trends

About a billion minutes have passed since Jesus walked the earth; in the next twelve years, one and a half billion babies will be born. The world population will not only be larger, but will be tilted toward the Pacific rim. It will also be an urban world with some twenty-two mega cities of ten million plus by the year 2000. It will become both an older and a younger world. In the first quarter of the 21st century there will be a billion people over sixty. And yet, sixty percent of the world's population is now under twenty-four. We can also expect the world to be in continuing conflict between ideologies, races, and classes. As conflict divides our world, communication is drawing it closer because of the information explosion. The information era is tending to divide people between the have's and the have nots.[8]

—Leighton Ford

Our society is changing rapidly, greatly impacting the church. Examining the literature of futurists brings even greater clarity and challenge to the macro-level changes occurring within our world. Issues include globalization where we are forced to compete in a global economy and cope with an emerging world order due to the falling of the Berlin Wall and the openness this brings to European culture and business. We cannot deny that the changing work force will continue to impact our world and our churches. The work force including both sexes in labor and management positions, flexible work hours, job sharing, and other trends will all impact society.[9] Then there is the issue of health care—its cost, the injustice of the system, and the ethical decisions brought about by medical advancements. David Floyd observed,

> The soaring costs of prolonging the lives of the very elderly will soon become unacceptable to society, but refusing them treatment that could preserve their lives for additional weeks, months, or possibly years will be equally unacceptable to many people.[10]

> The concept of death will be reevaluated in light of technologies
> that enable vital organs to function indefinitely. Even "brain
> death" may not be the final criterion for the end of human
> life.[11]

Technology will not only change medicine but our transportation
as well. Futurists are calling for personal rapid transit systems
featuring one- or two-passenger vehicles running on a network of
light rails with many more stations than today's mass-transit
systems.

George Barna, a Christian research analyst, makes the following observations in his book, *The Frog in the Kettle.* In the 1990s
in America,

- Materialism is in.
- Commitment is out.
- The quest for the best is rampant.
- Skepticism rules.
- Traditions are being questioned on every front.

Barna also examines the trends in the shaping of our family and
friends in the year 2000. His observations can be summarized in
the following statements.

- Serial monogamy will continue due to the AIDS virus.
- There will be a dramatic rise in the number of multigenerational
  homes
- Most people will acknowledge that they are likely to have several
  spouses over the course of a lifetime.
- Street gangs will provide a new form of family for many
  children, teens, and young adults.
- Many people can be characterized as lonely in the crowd.
- Child care will continue to boom as an industry due to dual
  working households and single-parent families.
- Elder care will blossom due to the aging population.
- Many people will be more apt to rent and lease in the 1990s, and
  there will be the introduction of cohousing among various
  generations.
- Friendships will be harder than ever to come by.

•More people will be working from their homes thanks to technological advances, job share programs, and other changes in the
workplace.

As if these changes in society were not enough for the church to
have to handle or learn to work within, Barna's research also
indicates the following changes that are certain to impact the
local church.

•Cohabitation will become more prevalent.
•New ideals and roles for women will continue to emerge.
•The family unit will continue to behave very differently. Family
members will spend less time together, meals are less likely to be
eaten at home as a shared family experience, and vacations will
be shorter and less likely to include all members of the family.
•Friendships will be desired but more difficult to engage in with
other persons due to mobility, cocooning, and other trends of
modern society.[12]

Kennon Callahan magnifies another issue the church must
not lose sight of in the world of the present and future: The
church no longer exists in a churchgoing society. The culture of
which we are a part is unchurched, a reality that has profound
implications for the work of the church—if indeed we see evangelism, mission, and/or ministry as part of the church's function
in society. Callahan indicates that in an unchurched culture
several factors must be noted:

•The value of church is not among the major values of the
culture.
•A substantial number of persons are not seeking out churches
on their own initiative.
•By and large, persons live life as though the church does not sub-
stantially matter. "People do not necessarily view the church as
harmful or hurtful. Rather, people simply view the church as not
particularly relevant or helpful."[13]

Many, if not most, of the trends I have summarized are already making their impact on the world and the church. The church, however, is looking everywhere else but inside itself to understand the reasons for the continuing decline of attendance and interest in church programs and ministries. We must examine the mission and function of the church. We must be willing to examine, kill, and bury some of our "sacred cows" (structures and philosophies that are now dated) if we are to minister effectively in the changing world. Robert Bellah revealed the potential impact of all these changes when he said,

> Our present situation requires an unprecedented increase in the ability to attend to new possibilities, moral as well as technical, and to put the new technical possibilities in a moral context. The challenges often seem overwhelming, but there are possibilities for an immense enhancement of our lives, individual and collective, based on a significant moral advance. One of the greatest challenges, especially for individualistic Americans, is to understand what institutions are—how we form them and how they in turn form us—and to imagine that we can actually alter them for the better.[14]

Bellah's advice certainly speaks to the church and its role in this changing world.

We must rediscover this basic biblical principle about the church: The functions of the local church must fit its mission, and its forms must follow its functions. Such a truth is so simple, yet very complex for the church that has focused more on the institution than on the mission. Paul Thigpen declares that this biblical truth has two applications: (1) The local church should abandon functions that have little to do with its mission in favor of those that do. (2) The local church should abandon forms that have become dysfunctional in favor of those that work.[15]

With all of this criticism of the local church, and all of the massive challenges before the church to minister in a changing world, should the church survive? If it does, what will the future church look like if it is to be effective?

For Reflection:

1. What are the values your church embraces most often?
2. What do you value most as a Christian leader in your church? In your world of work, play, community leadership, and so on?
3. Following Paul Thigpen's advice, what forms/structures should your local church abandon in order to become more kingdom-focused and effective in the 21st century?

The Future Church

The local church should and will survive if it realigns itself to the mission for which it was created. Westerhoff and Hughes provide insight into the nature of the church that will survive and transform the culture of which it is a part.

> The goal to remain in but not of the culture, so as to be a constant force of transformation, has been difficult to realize. While the culture expects that its religious communities will support and bless it, we contend that the church is intended to be what Walter Brueggemann describes as an alternative community with a counterconciousness. Only as such can the church contribute to the transformation of culture. A changed consciousness is more radical than political or economic change and more profound than social action. To change a people's consciousness is to reorder their reality. The church is to be an agent of transformation in society. It accomplishes this end by conforming its life to its story of transformation.[16]

(1) *The future church must be willing to allow the biblical text to speak by bringing the text and the people together over real-life situations.* As Linda Vogel said, "The story and vision of faith communities need to intersect with the experiences of individuals. . . . Learning by dialogue begins with what people know, rather than what they do not know. . . . It encourages participants to draw on past experiences and their future hopes as they attempt to share their own insights and questions and listen to the insights and questions of others."[17]

We must learn to be more relational in our teaching style. This is not to exclude the informational dimension, but it does suggest that we must become more relational in communicating our information around the "teachable moments" in an adult's life. Curriculum must help adults make sense out of life experiences and situations they encounter and also discover ways to respond that create satisfaction and hope rather than pain and despair.[18]

(2) *The future church must learn to acknowledge and work with the gathered church and the scattered church.* Over the last decades, most of our resources have been given to supporting the gathered church that meets at the church building on one or two days a week. This is certainly a needed dimension of church life, but it

does not fulfill the biblical function of the church. The Bible clearly declares that the people of God are dispersed into the world (the workplace, community functions, family life) during the week as the scattered church. We have virtually ignored the ministry of the scattered church. In future society the ministry of the scattered church will become critical to the church's survival and effectiveness. But how do we go about making this shift of emphasis?

We must learn to establish "come and go structures" within the design of church. We have pretty well mastered the "come structures." We develop a program and tell people to "come." In years past this has been sufficient, but in a time-poor society people are no longer coming to meetings that do not really meet their life needs. The challenge is to create "go structures" and affirm them as part of the church's ministry. This might be a social outing between nonchurchgoers and/or hurting persons with churchgoers. It might be blessing a nurse or firefighter for assisting in the redemptive work of the church as they do their daily work (even though they are not available to attend church meetings.) This will really challenge our thinking and planning!

We must also create accountability relationships that can support and facilitate the "go structures" and acknowledge and equip the scattered church. Simply stated, this is a covenantal relationship between two or more people that reflects grace, unit, and poise in the mutual accomplishing of a given task.[19]

(3) *The future church must be flexible in structure and leadership.* In his book, *User-Friendly Churches*, George Barna declares, "The ministry is not called to fit the church's structure; the structure exists to further effective ministry."[20] In *The Problem of Wineskins: Church Structure in a Technological Age*, Howard Snyder makes the following suggestions for the structure of the future church.

•The church must be structured so as to affirm the uniqueness and value of human personality. Church structure must make room for the individual if the mind of Christ is to become a reality in the church.

•Church structure must be flexible and varied. Church structure must provide a variety of outlets for ministry and expressing the meaning of faith in Christ.
•Church structure must help sustain a Christian's life in the world. The church's task is not to keep Christians off the streets but to send them out equipped for kingdom tasks.
•Church structure must be built upon spiritual gifts.[21]

Leaders in the future church must be enlisted according to their spiritual gifts and their calling. It is most important to this generation of adults that their time and resources be used to "make a difference." We will also see more leaders assigned to short-term program and ministry functions. Persons will give the church only so much time.

(4) *The future church will find its focus where form emerges with function.* For too long our forms have determined our function. The Scriptures have very little to say about the form the church should take, but it has a great deal to say about the function of the church. The historical-, traditional-, and family-prescribed forms have now almost robbed us from being about our biblical function. Again, we are found maintaining an institution rather than building a church.

(5) *The future church must become more relational and incarnational in its approach to church life and Christianity.* This relational model must permeate all aspects of the church—worship, Christian education, fellowship, training—so as to help persons learn again to be friendly and make friends. Since the open front porch and rocking chairs have disappeared from communities, and air conditioners have run us inside, we really are becoming a very lonely people, void of relationship-building skills. The church of all places must help.

We must further design experiences in which our faith life touches and impacts our real life—family, friends, work. The Word of God must "be made flesh" again as it intersects the lives of hurting, searching adults. Linda Vogel gives substance to this issue when she declares,

People who are contented with their lives are not very hungry. Those who want and need feeding generally have: (1) a disruption in their lives, (2) a need to reflect on their own experiences, (3) new ears for hearing the scriptures, (4) new eyes seeing connections between personal stories and the faith story, (5) a desire to celebrate through remembering and ritualizing, (6) a commitment to serve.[22]

(6) *Finally, the future church must become intentional about finding a balance between a program-based design and a ministry-based design.* (Note the comparison chart below.) If the church is to reach this changing world, it must stretch its definition of church beyond "ya'll come" programs to ministries that touch people and teach people where and when they hurt. This might be at the church, or it might be held in a local hotel, restaurant, community park, or other public place.

Program-Based Approach	**Ministry-Based Approach**
Concerned with programs	Concerned with people
Inward focus	Outward focus
Interested in "adding to the church"	Interested in making a difference in the world
Focuses on "doing church"	Balances "being"/"doing" church
Self-serving/maintenance-minded	Servant- and ministry-minded
Clergy primarily seek to activate churchgoing laity	Involves *all* God's people in mission and ministry
"Come structures" are the order of the day, encouraging people to serve within the institution	"Go structures" are encouraged and created to provide channels of ministry beyond the institution

For Reflection:

1. Review the previous chart and answer these questions:
   (a) Which side of the chart do you relate to most frequently?
   (b) What programs and events in your church can you list on each side of the chart? Make a list now.
   (c) What insights and realities have you discovered?
   (d) Who do you need to share these insights with? When will you do this?

Conclusion

Conversion begins with a point in time and unfolds through a series of events and experiences in which one encounters God and tastes reconciliation, comfort, hope, healing, and renewal. The conversion of the church will be no different. Hopefully, your encounter with issues raised in this book has provided an insight into the changes God may be calling you and your congregation to encounter.

Leaders today are having to learn to struggle with how to customize for their own cultures, to adjust to the world of "high tech/high touch" without jeopardizing the integrity and truth of the gospel. Such change requires reading, study, and ongoing reflection and support. The journey will require determination, great faith, risk, intentionality, and understanding that there are no more quick fixes nor easy mass-produced programs. Diversity has created much challenge and opportunity.

Many writers are challenging the church to renewal and response to cultural shifts. Particularly consider Bob Dale's leadership strategies. His chart helps summarize the shifts and also points us toward the next steps. His strategies can serve as a source of challenge for all Christian leaders to move beyond our comfort zones into effectiveness that is likely to stretch us in some painful ways. Bob Dale has raised significant issues specifically related to paradigm shifts we can no longer ignore if we desire effectiveness in our pagan and rapidly changing culture.

Also consider the following exercises to help insure greater effectiveness as we move into the 21st century.

- On the contents page check those issues you need to review, and circle those issues you need to discuss with other church leaders. List those fellow church leaders you need to dialogue with about this material.
- Invite other leaders to be a part of a learning community that meets to reflect on this material and other sources that might be helpful to move you forward. Consider facilitating this group. Be certain to notify your pastor and staff of your concern, interest, and plans.
- Commit to praying about issues you have encountered that are unclear or unsettling to you. Pray seeking God's direction,

affirmation, or clarification. Enlist other leaders to pray with and for you as you struggle with paradigm shifts and conversions that may be very foreign to your "churched culture" orientation or your generational comfort zones.

•Explore Robert Dale's paradigm shifts for Christian leaders (see the chart below). Check those you need to explore. Circle those your congregation needs to explore together. Share these insights with fellow leaders.

From . . .	To . . .
Management	Leadership
"Doing to"	"Discovering with"
Factories	Homes
Owners	Entrepreneurs
Skilled workers	Lifelong learners
Influence's levers	Meaning's symbols
Assumes progress	Assumes meaning
"If we build it, they will come and buy it"	"If we understand it, they will know . . . and value it"
Brawn	Brains
Position power	Personal power
National/Institutional	Global/Local
Gender-exclusive	Gender-inclusive
Physics metaphors	Biology metaphors
Scientific	Spiritual
Technological	Artistic
Rational	Nonrational
Top-down	Bottom-up

I would enjoy and benefit from hearing from you about your learnings, struggles, and insights. Thanks for sharing this part of my journey and for your commitment to helping lead the church toward conversion. Contact me at the following address:

Edward Hammett
P.O. Box 1107
Cary NC 27513-1107
(E-mail) CompuServe 73752,3377

For Reflection:

1. What has the Spirit said to you as a result of your encounter with this book?

2. What is the Spirit calling you to do with the new insights, burdens, and challenges you have?

3. What are the next steps the Spirit of Christ is calling you to take? Write the steps here. List dates, times, and people beside each step to insure that you move forward.

4. What place do you hold in helping the church become more effective in the 21st century?

Notes

[1]Dietrich Bonhoeffer, *Letters and Papers from Prison* (New York: Macmillan, 1967) 211.

[2]Howard Snyder, *Radical Renewal* (Downers Grove IL: InterVarsity Press, 1975) 16.

[3]Ibid., 52.

[4]Ibid., 59.

[5]Ibid., 66.

[6]John Havlick, *People-Centered Evangelism* (Nashville TN: Broadman Press, 1971) 47.

[7]John Westerhoff and Caroline Hughes, *On the Threshold of God's Future* (San Francisco: Harper & Row, 1986) 41.

[8]Leighton Ford, *Transformational Leadership* (Downers Grove IL: InterVarsity Press, 1991) 20-21.

[9]Michael Marien, *Future Survey*, January–July 1991 (Maryland: World Future Society) 2.

[10]David Floyd, *The Futurist*, July/August 1991 (Maryland: World Future Society) 35.

[11]Ibid., November/December 1990, 37.

[12]George Barna, *The Frog and the Kettle* (Ventura CA: Regal Publishers, 1990) 32-37, 67-77.

[13]Kennon Callahan, *Effective Church Leadership* (San Francisco: Harper & Row, 1990) 19-20.

[14]Robert Bellah, *The Good Society* (New York: Knopf, 1991) 5.

[15]Paul Thigpen, "What is a Local Church to Do?" *Discipleship Journal* (1992)69: 33-34.

[16]Westerhoff and Hughes, 70-71.

[17]Linda Vogel, *Teaching and Learning in Communities of Faith* (San Francisco: Jossey-Bass, 1991) 65.

[18]Ibid., 15-16.

[19]Max DePree, *Leadership Is an Art* (East Lansing MI: Michigan State University Press, 1987) 55-56.

[20]Barna, 137.

[21]Snyder, 122-27.

[22]Vogel, 15-16.

Appendixes

Needs Assessment

Please complete and return this survey to:

Laity Leadership Development Team
P.O. Box 1107
Cary NC 27512-1107

Prioritize needs or situations with which you would like help (1–I encounter most frequently; 2–I encounter occasionally; 3–I least encounter, but would like help with).

__Unwed couples living together, attending church
__Unwed parents requesting parent/baby dedication
__Interracial/biracial marriages/relationships
__Non-Christians in active church leadership roles
__Same sex marriages/relationships
__Divorce/remarriage of clergy/church leaders
__Time-poor families/leaders
__Coping with secular culture
    __Values
    __Ethics
    __Definition of family
    __Capitalism
    __Consumerism
    __Parenting
    __Value and use of money
    __Other
__Gender role confusion in society and church
__Other

Avenues for training in which you would most likely participate (1–most likely; 2–possibly; 3–least likely)

__Seminars in my church
__Interactive computer seminar or computer programs
__Program learning via video or audio tape presentations
__Teleconferencing to a local community college
__Regional or statewide conferencing
__Learning clusters of laypersons and/or clergy, led by a provided facilitator, who are dealing with similar issues

__Learning clusters of laypersons and/or clergy who are dealing with similar issues and are from the same type of church (i.e. size, demographics, region of state, culture)

__"Teaching churches" where a church experienced in dealing with a given issue mentors a church currently dealing with that issue

__Other

Thanks for your valuable insights! If you would like survey results or a follow-throuh contact, please give the following information.

Name_____

Address_____

Phone_____

The Stewardship of Life
Telling the Story; Strengthening the Mission

Objectives
1. To provide tools for sharing the story of God's movement in your life
2. To provide a forum for experiencing other people's stories and an opportunity to refine your storytelling skills
3. To connect your story to the Christian story as a celebration of God's mission

Biblical Overview
Session Outline
I. Why Your Story Is Important (John 15:5, 8).
   A. You are God's instrument (John 3:16, 17).
   B. You are a pathway for God's ministry (Ephesians 4:1 1f).
   C. You are called to be a blessing (Genesis 12).
   D. You are called to be God's representative in this world (1 Peter 2:9-10; John 14:31; 17:11).

II. Why Telling Your Story Is Important and Life-Changing (John 15:5)
   A. Your life experiences are under God's watchcare (Exodus 3).
   B. Your obedience activates God's power (John 15:9-13).
   C. God calls you to be salt, light, and leaven in the world (Matthew 5:13-15).
   D. God calls you to share God's love and to be obedient vessels and partners in the divine mission (Matthew 28:19f; 10:6-7).

III. How Your Story Can Strengthen God's Mission in Your Church, Area, State, and World (John 15:15; 17:11, 18-19; Acts 1:8; 2 Corinthians 5:18-21)
   A. God calls you to be a partner in God's mission.
   B. God empowers by Presence, Spirit, and role model.
   C. Your story is a pathway for God's revelation to and working in the world.
   D. God's call is for you to be a witness and partner in the ministry and message of reconciliation in the world.
   E. Your experience of God in the world is evidence of God's working in your life and in the world.

IV. What Makes a Good Story (John 4; Exodus 3)
 A. An encounter—Where do you encounter God or the things of God?
 B. An interpretation—What does this experience say to you about who God is and/or how God works?
 C. An evaluation—What biblical/theological truths inform and clarify your experience and/or interpretation?
 D. A challenge—What is God challenging or calling you to be or do because of this encounter?

V. Discovering Places to Tell Your Story (John 3:16; Matthew 28:19f)
 A. Go into all the world.
 B. Share as you go about daily activities.
 C. Do all that you do for the glory of God.
 D. Be attentive to God's leading.
 E. Watch for cues that might indicate God's leading.
 F. Listen for open doors in talking with others.

VI. The Fruit of Storytelling (John 15:5, 7, 8, 15, 16)
 A. It informs others of God's working in and through you.
 B. It creates opportunity for God to work.
 C. It shines the light of divine truth in dark places.
 D. It offers guidance to the searching.
 E. It motivates others to obedience, giving, and faithfulness.

Preparing to Tell Your Story

Session Outline

I.   What encounters/experiences have you had that have helped form your ideas about and relationship with God?

II. What insights and truths did you discover in or because of these experiences?

III. What made these experiences possible?
   A. People
   B. Institutions
   C. The Spirit's leading/presence
   D. Resources
   E. Other

IV. What truths/insights have you held onto that can benefit others? How can you most effectively relay these experiences?

V.   What dots need to be placed, labeled, and connected to insure effective, powerful storytelling? (Identify the dots, place the dots on a timeline or a potential picture format, and begin to find ways of connecting these dots for effective communication. The dots are to represent the various insights collected in the above questions/reflections.)

VI. How have you felt, and what have you learned through this experience? What meaning has been revived or renewed through this experience?

VI. Where are the places, and who are the people God is leading you to share this story with in the near future?

VII. How can we help you complete this process so that God might be glorified and the divine mission strengthened?

Activating the Process of Discipleship

Explanation: Assessing spiritual maturity is such a personal issue that many have avoided the subject. However, such avoidance only leads to apathy, drifting, and misdirection for the church and/or the struggling Christian. The following stages and indicators are not intended to be exhaustive, but rather suggestive and directive.

Instructions: Read through each descriptive stage and the accompanying indicators for assessing your spiritual maturity. After reading through each section, reread the indicators and check those that are indicative of your present lifestyle and commitment.

Stage One—Experience Discovery
(Come and See)

Basic Description: Providing entry points that offer the non-believer opportunities to express initial interest in and an introduction to Christ.

Indicators
__I am questioning life's purpose and/or meaning of events/experiences.
_I have a growing awareness of my inadequacy and sinfulness.
_I am seeking a way to connect with a church family and/or those who care about me.
_I am seeking authentic relationships with others and with Christ.
_I have a growing hunger for truth.

Resources
Survival Kit for New Christians (Ralph Neighbor)
Forever Beginning (Donald Shelby)
Learning to Walk with God (Charlie Riggs)
Taking Next Steps (Ralph Hodge and Jerre Herring)
Workbook on Becoming Alive in Christ (Maxie Dunman)
Remembering Your Story (Richard Morgan)

Assignments
1. Seek out a church and/or a Christian to dialogue with about your questions and concerns.
2. Read 1 John in the Bible.

Stage Two—Experience Belonging
(Come and Follow Me)

Basic Description: Helping new believers and other new church members connect with the church's theological and historical identity, as well as socially and emotionally through intentional assimilation in and through relation-oriented support structures.

Indicators
_I understand the purpose of the church.
_I am excited about growing in Christ with these people.
_I am finding clarity about what God wants me to do in ministry to and with others.
_I participate in a small group (Sunday School, another church program, support group) on a regular (three times a month) basis.
_I feel that I have a place in this body of believers and desire to fulfill that function through the recognition and use of my gifts.

Resources
Survival Kit for New Christians (Ralph Neighbor)
Your Life and Your Church (James L. Sullivan)
Jesus on Leadership (Gene Wilkes)
Biblical Basis of Missions (Avery Willis)
Alone with God (Delbene/Montgomery)
The Workbook on the Christian Walk (Maxie Dunman)

Assignments
1. Explore the life of your congregation through personal observation, interviews with church leaders, and a new member orientation process.
2. Participate in a small group on a regular basis.
3. Invite an experienced member or fellow new member to have lunch and discuss what God is doing in your lives.

Stage Three—Experience Empowerment
(Come and Be with Me)

Basic Description: Engaging in spiritual life directions through disciplines that enhance the development of an inward journey that prepares one to lead others into a deeper relationship with and commitment to Christ.

Indicators
_I am involved in a daily prayer life seeking to find focus and empowerment for my ministry.
_I am involved in a consistent study of the Scriptures.
_I am engaged in regular fellowship with other believers seeking to find God at work in our lives.
_I am opening my life to others who can help me achieve the spiritual growth I'm seeking.
_I am intentional about finding a quiet time with God when I can talk and listen to God.
_I am seeking to invest my life in the spiritual growth of at least one other person on a regular basis
.

Resources
Living Your Christian Values (Ralph Neighbor)
How to Study Your Bible (Thomas Lea)
Disciple's Prayer Life (Catherine Walker and T. W. Hunt)
The Mind of Christ (T. W. Hunt)
MasterLife (Avery Willis)
Experiencing God (Claude King and Henry Blackaby)
The Workbook on Love, the Jesus Way (Maxie Dunman)
Shaped by the Word (M. Robert Mulholland, Jr.)

Assignments
1. Enlist a trustworthy fellow believer who can hold you accountable in your spiritual life goals.
2. Meet regularly with this person to assess your growth needs.

Stage Four—Experience Mission
(Come Abide in Me)

Basic Description: Engaging in spiritual life disciplines that enhance the development of an outward journey and equip leaders to lead others in aligning their lives with God's plan to impact the world for Christ.

Indicators
__I am finding guidance, motivation, and encouragement for ministry and daily life through my devotional and prayer life.
__I am discovering a growing burden for people, events, and circumstances around me.
__I sense that God is empowering and calling me to minister in areas of brokenness in my world (home, work, leisure, church).
__I am finding that I'm more concerned about issues and people outside the church walls than those inside the church walls.
__I am intentionally seeking to build witnessing and/or ministering relationships with hurting and lost persons in my daily work and play.
__I am committed to helping fellow Christians hear the needs of the broken in the world.
__I am willing to open myself to fellow Christians who can hold me accountable for being faithful in my ministry.

Resources
Fresh Encounter with God (Henry Blackaby)
Discovering the Depths (William Clemmons)
LifeAnswers: Making Sense of Your World (Ken Hemphill)
Learning to Listen (Wendy Miller)
Daily Secrets of Christian Living (Andrew Murray)
Discovery Sunday (Herb Miller)
The Hunger of the Heart (Ron Delbene)

Assignments
1. Do the ministry that you believe God has given you.
2. Meet weekly with a spiritual guide/mentor to help you discern and prepare for the ministry opportunities you find before you.